SCRAP QUILTS

TECHNIQUES PLUS PATTERNS
OLD AND NEW
FOR MAKING QUILTS
FROM COLLECTED FABRICS

by Judy Martin

M.Q.M.

Moon Over the Mountain Publishing Company
in association with
Quilter's Newsletter Magazine

AUTHOR'S ACKNOWLEDGMENTS

This book was written in connection with my work at *QUILTER'S NEWSLETTER MAGAZINE*, and I thank the rest of the art and editorial staff for their invaluable help to me in its production. Special thanks to Bonnie Leman, Mary Leman Austin, Louise O. Townsend, Marie Shirer, Jerry DeFelice, Laurie Meador, and Andrew H. Leman. Thanks also to Kathy Dubois, Vivian Ritter, Marla Gibbs Stefanelli, Carol Crowley, and Ivy Malden.

I also want to thank the quiltmakers who worked so hard to help me finish the quilts on time to appear in this book: Brenda Bain, Catherine S. Chase, Reni Dieball, Ann Elliott, Berniece Fair, Juanita Froese, Jeanette Goodrich, Susan Harringa, Shirley Ann Holbrook, Jeri Hoffmeyer, Judy Leo, Jackie Madison, Louise Morrison, Gloria Oliver, Carol Sears, Mina Slade, Marie Shirer, Marla Gibbs Stefanelli, Phyllis Street, Louise O. Townsend, Geri Waechter, Hella Wagner, Margaret Waltz, and Shirley Wegert.

Also due my thanks are the people who shared quilts or photographs of quilts: Minako Abe, Lou Ann Buss, Rebekah Clark, Michael Kile and Roderick Kirakofe of The Quilt Digest Press, Jill Liddell, Nancy Krickbaum, Eugenia Mitchell, Cyril Nelson of E. P. Dutton, Inc., Marina Ratliff, Nancy Rose, Yuko Watanabe of *Patchwork Tsushin*, and Diane Wold.
...J. M.

Photographs by Jerry DeFelice

Settings and furnishings for photos on front and back covers and on page 63 courtesy of: The Yacht Club and Charter Oak, Inc. Denver, Colorado

EDITOR'S ACKNOWLEDGMENTS

Since the early 1970s when the current quilt revival began, people have been actively collecting fabric for quilts. Many people collected it faster than they could use it up in quilts, and by 1984 the stacks of prints in closets and attics was an inside joke among "fabriholics." It seemed the time was right for a series on Scrap Quilts in *QUILTER'S NEWSLETTER MAGAZINE*. What better way to help our readers use their fabric stashes (and give them an excuse to collect more) than with the very special quilts that have always been America's favorites? So, with the February, 1984, issue of *QNM*, we started a monthly feature entitled "Scrap Quilts." Readers responded with enthusiasm and told us they'd like even more Scrap Quilt ideas. This book resulted.

It needs to be noted here, along with my appreciation to her, that Judy Martin not only wrote the book but also designed its layout, designed and cut out seventeen quilts especially for it, pieced two of the quilts, quilted a third, and pieced a block or section of most of the others. My thanks also to my hardworking and talented staff already mentioned for help all along the way.
...Bonnie Leman

CONTENTS

COLOR PLATES

PATTERN INDEX

INTRODUCTION

Ask anyone to think of a quilt. What does he or she visualize? Probably a Log Cabin, Double Wedding Ring, Nine-Patch, Tumbling Blocks, or other SCRAP QUILT.

THE SENTIMENTAL FAVORITE. Steeped in tradition, totally typical yet absolutely one of a kind, the scrap quilt is the most quilt-like and the best loved of quilts.

For quiltmakers and quilt lovers alike, the scrap quilt has an undeniable emotional appeal. Each fabric calls up memories—cousin Mary's Easter dress, Aunt Eva's kitchen curtains, Grandma's apron, the blouse you wore when you were seven. Your scrap quilt is made using bits and pieces from your daily life, and it reflects you and the people and things meaningful to you. It has a beauty from within; it pulls at the heart-strings; it warms both body and soul.

THE ULTIMATE BEAUTY. Sentiment aside, scrap quilts can also be among the most graphically stunning of quilts. A rich tapestry of print and pattern is woven into the warp of the design, adding surface interest, bringing out secondary motifs, playing up the block here and the overall pattern there, lending depth to the color scheme, and inviting close inspection. Rhythmic without being repetitive, the scrap quilt is as interesting to look at as it is to make.

A JOY TO MAKE. Whether you are a novice or an expert quiltmaker, you'll have fun making scrap quilts. Because the variety of prints and colors used in a scrap quilt adds so much visual interest, attractive (even stunning) scrap quilts can be made from the most basic patterns. Simple Nine-Patches, Log Cabins, or Variable Stars in scraps make marvelous first quilts. You don't need to be an artist to make a beautiful and creative scrap quilt. As you can see from the photographs in this book, just about any quilt pattern can be made in scraps—not just the Double Wedding Rings and Grandmother's Flower Gardens that you've seen so many times before. Patterns as diverse as Irish Chain, Storm at Sea, or the pieced and appliquéd Arrowroot all make great scrap quilts. You can add your own touch to a favorite traditional pattern simply by interpreting it in scraps. And you don't need hard-and-fast rules for design and fabric place-ment. A few common-sense guidelines are all you need to know to get started.

Your first scrap quilt will provide plenty of experience in playing with fabric combinations, giving you a good feel for how scraps work together. You may make a few "mistakes" at first; but you'll learn from them, and a few small goofs will never be detected in the myriad combinations and recombinations of fabrics in the whole quilt. With the design and sewing end of the project kept simple, you can concentrate your full attention on the really fun part: collecting fabrics, sorting them, and playing with various combina-tions of them.

Easy to master yet always a challenge,

the scrap quilt lures us with its simplicity, and it continues to fascinate us with its delightful graphic complexity.

SOMETHING FOR NOTHING. For some of us, the economy of using scrap-bag snippets, cutting remnants, and odd lots to make a quilt is appealing if not a financial necessity. A scrap quilt can be made for little more than the cost of the batting and lining. That's not just something for nothing—that's something-really-special for nothing.

A QUILTER'S ANTHOLOGY. If you are a long-time quiltmaker—and you've stopped making clothes somehow over the years—you probably used up your true scraps years ago. Even so, your "scrap" quilts can be full of wonderful memories if you make them from yardage stockpiled over the years. One keepsake scrap quilt will call up memories of the many quilts you've made and long since parted with. In a sense it can be an album or anthology, a personal record of your other quilts.

Besides the quilts brought to mind, there are other memories saved in scrap quilts from stockpiled yardage: you may recognize a fabric you brought home from a visit with Mother; the piece saved from your high-school days; the paisley your husband gave you for your birthday the first year you were married; the one you wrangled from Lucy by swapping some of the red print she admired. Images of people and places, moments out of your past not unlike the memories called up by a piece of your sister's dress or your daughter's playsuit, are preserved in these collected fabrics, as well.

A FABRIHOLIC'S PERFECT EXCUSE. For the fabric lovers and collectors of the world (fabriholics)—and I know there are a lot of us—scrap quilts can be very special, indeed. The sheer variety of fabrics in one of these quilts is fascinating to behold. Furthermore, making scrap-type quilts offers the perfect opportunity for using the myriad fabrics you have collected over the years without (heaven forbid!) using them up entirely. Scrap quilts offer a kind of economy, too: They free space in your fabric cupboards, and they let you use pieces that may not fit in with your current tastes. Scrap quilts provide justification for the fabric you have bought and an excuse to buy more, for a good collection of fabrics—whether it is built upon years of scrimping and saving to buy a bit here and there, carefully budgeted and planned purchases, or wild binges and spending sprees—is the cornerstone of every successful scrap quilt. Because you need a broad selection of fabrics to make even one scrap quilt, excess yardage and rejects from other projects can be thought of as welcome additions to your collection rather than errors in judgement. And buying with no particular project in mind need not make you feel guilty when you are "building your collection" for scrap quilts.

If you make only one quilt in your lifetime, make it a scrap quilt. Although there are many other types of beautiful quilts to be made and enjoyed, no other single kind offers so much in one project: sentiment, memories, beauty, fun, creative stimulation, documentation, and practicality. But chances are, if you make one scrap quilt you'll soon want to make another, and another.

SCRAP QUILTS THEN & NOW

Scrap quilts were born of necessity. The Orlofskys suggest in *Quilts in America* that patchwork was a natural extension of mending and the mind-set of the women who were forced by circumstances to exercise frugality: "Patching of clothing—and of course, bedcoverings—was a common and necessary technique. The idea of using saved scraps of materials in piecing was also natural to the Puritan and frontier mentality of thrift, utility, and economy."[1] Carrie Hall, in *The Romance of the Patchwork Quilt in America,* describes the situation:

> *The pieced quilt was familiar to most households where economy was a necessity, as it was created of scraps of material not otherwise of use. The pieced quilt in pioneer days provided means of turning to good account the precious scraps of printed cottons, at that period so rare and costly.*[2]

While it is true that scrap quilts today are often made from new fabrics and with careful planning and obvious interest in the graphic effect, it is an oversimplification to say that *then* scrap quilts were just a necessity and *now* they are an art form. Scrap quilts today are still made out of thrift sometimes, the maker being motivated by circumstances or by a sense of economy. And quilt historians agree that, as soon as fabrics became affordable, women spiced up their scrap collections with purchased yardage or did whatever they could to carry out a planned pattern. Patricia Mainardi, in her 1973 essay "Quilts, The Great American Art," wrote:

> *It is interesting to note that there are few quilts, even among the crazy quilts, totally lacking in a sense of design, for virtually immediately women began the process of making their quilts beautiful as well as useful. With the same poverty of means, but the addition of a sense of design, women began to cut their scraps into patches of uniform size and shape (the Hit an' Miss pattern), or to sew all the light-colored ones into one strip, the dark ones into another and alternate the strips (the Roman Stripe pattern). . . . As the quilt designs evolved, women went to greater pains to have their quilts fulfill their conceptions: they traded fabric scraps with other quilt makers, dyed some to obtain the shades they wanted, and embroidered on the plain homespun if that was all they had.*[3]

The Orlofskys tell us that because of the Industrial Revolution, by 1850 materials had become affordable and available enough that "materials were bought specifically for the purpose of making a quilt. The housewife was no longer dependent upon the accumulation of scraps of different colors and sizes in her scrap bag to create a specific pattern or design. She was now able to repeat a pattern in a particular color of fabric to carry out a desired color scheme."[4] But the scrap quilt survived. As they go on to say, "Quilts were to become less a salvage art than they had been, though economy and thrift were too engrained in the American character to be totally forgotten."[5]

Surely the Puritan ethic figures somewhat in the continued popularity of scrap quilts, but

1. Patsy and Myron Orlofsky, *Quilts in America* (New York: McGraw-Hill, 1974), p. 12.
2. Carrie A. Hall and Rose G. Kretsinger, *The Romance of the Patchwork Quilt in America* (New York: Bonanza Books, 1935), p. 15.

3. Patricia Mainardi, *Quilts: The Great American Art* (San Pedro, CA: Miles & Weir, Ltd., 1978), p. 19. Originally published in *The Feminist Art Journal* 2, No. 1 (Winter 1973).
4. Orlofsky, *Op. cit.,* p. 58.
5. *Ibid.*

then, as now, another aspect peculiar to scrap quilts may be even more responsible for the ongoing appeal: Scrap quilts have great emotional significance. Scrap fabrics call up memories—associations with people and places meaningful to us. Elaine Hedges notes in *American Quilts: A Handmade Legacy* that in the days before photographs were commonplace, "fabric scraps and the quilts made from them were what photographs would be to a family today: they verified existence and became the loving ties that bound. They were tactile communication and reassurance."[6]

In the same museum catalog Hedges describes a set of letters now in the possession of the Nebraska State Historical Society:

The correspondence among Hannah, several of the daughters, and Margaret is a moving record of the way in which fabrics and quilts bound together members of a dispersed family.

"I have been looking for something to send you, but I could not find anything that I could send in a letter bitt [sic] a piece of my new dress..." Hannah writes to Margaret from Wisconsin in 1850. As the correspondence proceeded throughout the 1850s and 1860s, the sending of dress scraps from mother to daughter, and from sister to sister, continued: "Here is a piece of my gingham Lydia made me"; "a piece of my dress of delanes"; "a piece of my bonnet, trimmed with green plaid ribbon"; and finally, "I will send you some pieces of my new dresses for patch work." In 1865, a sister, Amelia, wrote to Margaret, "Hear [sic] are some peaces [sic] for Mary's quilt." The family also exchanged quilt blocks, and sent each other samples of calico to be matched for use in a quilt.[7]

An April 1888 *Good Housekeeping* article by Annie Curd (quoted in Jeannette Lasanky's *In The Heart of Pennsylvania* catalog) tells of the emotional appeal of scrap quilts:

I have found nothing so desirable for summer covers as the old fashioned scrap quilt, of which our mothers and grandmothers were so proud.... Every young girl should piece one quilt at least to carry away with her to her husband's home, and if her lot happens to be cast among strangers, as is often the case, the quilt when she unfolds it will seem like the face of a familiar friend, and will bring up a whole host of memories of mother, sister, friend, too sacred for us to intrude upon.[8]

This emotional content figured in the immense popularity of certain kinds of scrap quilts at various historical junctures. In the Victorian era, and again in the 1920s, a special kind of scrap quilt was popular, the Charm Quilt. Cuesta Benberry in *Quilter's Newsletter Magazine* tells us that a Charm Quilt was "a pieced quilt in which no two patches were cut of the same fabric, and it was set block to block with no sashing."[9] Women used their own scraps and traded for others, often taking "longer to accumulate the necessary assortment of scraps than it did to make the quilt."[10] She goes on to say that "A Charm Quilt was a very personal type of quilt—more a curiosity than a beauty; more an album of fabrics of the time than a clearly defined patterned quilt top."[11]

Earlier, the Friendship Quilt enjoyed popularity. The quiltmaker incorporated scraps from the dresses of her friends, with a different friend represented by each block, and the blocks all of the same design.

Memory or mourning quilts, pieced out of the clothing of a friend or relative who has died, were popular at one time, as well, and are occasionally made today. Radka Donnell, a contemporary quiltmaker who appeared in the film "Quilts In Women's Lives," describes helping a mother work through her grief over the loss of her daughter by piecing the daughter's clothes into a scrap quilt.[12]

The scraps used in old quilts give clues to the periods in which the quilts were made. In the last half of the 19th century, block patterns such as Bear's Paw, Lemoyne Star, and Carpenter's Wheel were favored. These were made in the turkey reds, bright yellow-oranges, indigo blues, and browns widely available at that time. During the Great Depression, when scrap quilts were revived as a source of pleasure and functional necessity in hard times, cheery pastels in Dresden Plate, Fan, and Grandmother's Flower Garden prevailed.

Now, the wide availability of fabrics and colors permits us to make scrap quilts of every description. Contemporary scrap quilts can have a richer look than ever before because today's quiltmakers have a much wider variety of prints and colors available to them than quiltmakers of yesteryear.

But scrap quilts, both then and now, rise above their function and their humble origin to shine with the creativity of their makers and to glow with their own special stories. The reverence of many quiltmakers today for the beautiful scrap quilts of the past figures in the great popularity of traditional patterns for today's scrap quilts. However, contemporary works of original themes are also being made from scraps by many quilters. Lucky are tomorrow's quilters to have them both as a heritage.

6. L. T. Frye, Ed., *American Quilts: A Handmade Legacy* (Oakland, CA: The Oakland Museum, 1981), p. 64.

7. *Ibid.*, pp. 63-64.
8. Jeannette Lasansky, *In the Heart of Pennsylvania* Lewisburg, PA: Oral Traditions Project, 1985), p. 75.

9. Cuesta Benberry, "Charm Quilts," *Quilter's Newsletter Magazine* 11, No. 3 (March 1980), p. 14.
10. *Ibid.*
11. *Ibid.*
12. Frye, *Op. cit., p. 73.*

PLATE I: Bear's Paw Variation, 80″ x 78″, 1875-1890, from the Levi Strauss & Company art collection. Each block is different, made from scraps of many colors that seem to have been selected at random. The multicolored blocks are unified and framed by the cheerful blue borders and sashing. The contrast between a single, mid-range blue print and the strong prints in unexpected colors is very pleasing. Pattern is on page 30. (Photo courtesy of The Quilt Digest Press.)

PLATE II: Carpenter's Wheel, 104″ x 102″, 1835-1845. The stuffed leaves rise above a closely quilted background to give dramatic texture to this otherwise simple quilt. The quiltmaker chose to place a chintz flower block in the center, and its printed leaves tie in beautifully with the quilting. The colors must have been much brighter when the quilt was new over a century ago, but even now the quilt has a comfortable look anyone would enjoy. (Photo from America Hurrah Antiques courtesy E. P. Dutton, Inc. Quilt now in private collection.)

PLATE III: Devil's Puzzle, a Drunkard's Path variation, 88" x 97", pieced by Martha Fuerst and her niece Ruby McReynolds, circa 1930; quilted by Ruby's daughter, Nancy Krickbaum, 1984. Ruby's husband always laughed that with every new shipment of fabric into Scottsbluff, Nebraska, he knew that she would be out shopping for new quilt materials, and the myriad of prints in this quilt is testimony to her collecting instincts. Her name for the quilt was found on the outside of an envelope containing a few more patches that had been cut out but didn't fit into the quilt.

PLATE IV: Delectable Mountains Variation, 43″ x 77″, 1984, by Minako Abe, Japan. Delectable Mountains is a traditional American quilt pattern that Minako has succeeded in using in an original way. She decided to put as many colors into her quilt as possible. She did not preselect or sort the scraps—with the result that the quilt has an uncontrived look that is most refreshing. To complete the piece, she used several quilting patterns that do not attempt to follow the construction of the patchwork, and this creates additional texture. (Information courtesy Jill Liddell; photograph courtesy Yuko Watanabe and *Patchwork Tsushin,* Tokyo.)

PLATE V: Prairie Star, 88" x 88", 1984, by Lou Ann Buss. Lou Ann's inspiration was an antique quilt owned by the Camden County (New Jersey) Historical Society. Each of the large stars is a 16" block; the stars in the sashing are 4"; and the setting rectangles are a scant 1" wide. Lou Ann made the stars with a machine technique known as strip piecing. The background color was originally white, but after completing several blocks, Lou Ann thought the white was too stark. She solved the problem by tea-dyeing them in her microwave. Then she tea-dyed the rest of the white prints before piecing the remaining blocks. Lou Ann says, "I love scrap quilts, and as a beginning quilter I feel I can learn more about color and design by using a variety of fabrics."

PLATE VI: Op-Ex, 45″ ▶ x 45″, 1984, made by Nancy Rose using a 7½″ block in the traditional Flying Geese Pattern. Nancy wanted a contemporary graphic effect in this quilt. She achieved it by making the blocks from contrasting scraps and setting them solid to juxtapose the prints. The overall Flying Geese pattern still emerges but in a subtle and interesting way that modernizes its look. (Photo by Gil Rose.)

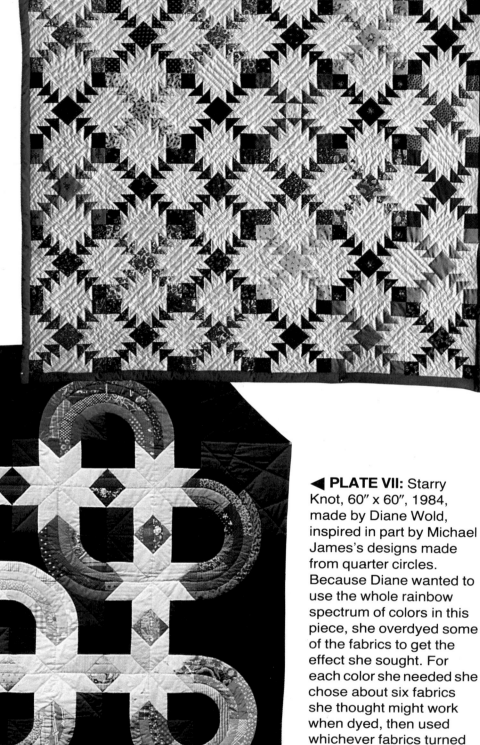

◀ **PLATE VII:** Starry Knot, 60″ x 60″, 1984, made by Diane Wold, inspired in part by Michael James's designs made from quarter circles. Because Diane wanted to use the whole rainbow spectrum of colors in this piece, she overdyed some of the fabrics to get the effect she sought. For each color she needed she chose about six fabrics she thought might work when dyed, then used whichever fabrics turned out best. She saved the leftovers for future scrap quilts. (Photo courtesy of Diane Wold.)

PLATE IX: Scrap Song, 45″ x 57″, ▶
by Marina Ratliff, 1984. This was
one of Marina's first scrap quilts,
made by her in a workshop led by
Nancy Halpern. She hand-dyed
some of the fabrics to add to the
color mix of scraps she had on
hand. (Photograph courtesy of
Marina Ratliff.)

▼ **PLATE VIII:** Crown of Thorns,
56″ x 56″, 1984, made by Rebekah
Clark. She divided fabrics from her
collection into lights and darks;
then her only established criterion
for the blocks was to use lights in
the points. Once the blocks were
complete, she moved them around
to choose an arrangement. (Photograph courtesy of Rebekah Clark.)

PLATE X: Detail, Maltese Circles (page 61).

PLATE XI: Detail, Op-Ex (page 14).

PLATE XII: Detail, Colorado Log Cabin (page 62).

PLATE XIII: Detail, Yank's Irish Chain (page 63).

PLATE XIV: Detail, Country Cousin (page 64).

PLATE XV: Detail, Stacked Bricks (page 40).

COLLECTING SCRAP FABRICS

Because new fabrics were scarce in pioneer America, scrap quilts were a way of "making do," with quiltmakers salvaging anything still serviceable from old clothes (and reusing bits from tattered quilts). In order to fill out their "palettes," they swapped with friends. But today, most of us value our time too much to spend hours and hours sewing a quilt from fabric already half worn out. Besides, the denims, double knits, interlocks, and synthetic blends that are omnipresent in today's clothing are not the preferred fabrics of quiltmakers. Today, scrap quilts are seldom second-quality quilts made from old castoffs.

Now, quilters make scrap quilts not for their economy so much as for their breathtaking beauty, visual complexity, old-fashioned charm, and sentiment. Many make scrap quilts from all new yardage or from unused fabric stockpiled over the years. Others make quilts with cutting remnants from sewing projects, perhaps supplemented with new yardage to fill in where needed. Either way, the quilts are charming and durable enough to last a long time. Scraps need not be acquired at great expense to be good, but any pieces of dubious quality—those that are weak from wear, faded, flimsy, coarse, or not colorfast—should be avoided. If you make quilts for the joy of the activity and the beauty of the finished product, you can multiply both the joy and the beauty by using good fabrics.

SELECTING THE BEST FABRICS FOR THE JOB.

Most quiltmakers prefer 100% cotton in a shirting or dress weight, such as broadcloth. Some quilters find cotton blends perfectly acceptable, although the blends do not turn under neatly for hand appliqué and some of them are transparent enough to reveal the seams of patchwork. For piecing, the decision to incorporate blends is largely a matter of personal taste. Do be sure to choose washable fabrics of similar weights. Avoid sheers, loosely or exceptionally tightly woven fabrics, limp, stretchy, thick, terribly wrinkly, or ravelly fabrics, except for special effects when you have taken into consideration the shortcomings of the fabric and made allowances for them. For example, you might want to make an all-corduroy quilt, but you should take deeper seam allowances to lessen the danger of ravelling, and you should plan to tie rather than quilt the piece because of its thickness.

BUILDING A COLLECTION OF FABRICS.

There are ways to come up with good materials, no matter what your financial circumstances are. The notion of "quilting on the halves" has been around for a long time, and it would be easy to arrange today. A quilter who can't afford materials simply quilts a top for someone else in exchange for the materials to make another for herself. That's twice as much work, you say? Maybe, but your quilt will last twice as long as one made from half-worn scraps, and it will be so much prettier, too.

If you can scrape together good materials to make one beautiful quilt to sell, the proceeds should enable you to buy materials for two or three quilts you can keep.

And, of course, you can keep your eyes open for every opportunity to salvage a good piece here and another there. Still, if circumstances permit, buying a new piece now and then will be a great advantage in making your scrap quilt sparkle with your own special individuality. The more varied and plentiful the scraps in your collection, the richer and finer your scrap quilts will be.

Here are a few suggestions for building a workable collection of fabrics for scrap quilts:

1. Tell your friends and neighbors that you would appreciate any cutting scraps from their sewing projects.

2. Investigate garage sales, estate sales, and auctions. Often unused fabric remnants can be found for pennies.

3. Save scraps from your own sewing projects, including the quilts you've made over the years.

4. Buy new yardage as you can afford it, whenever new fabrics come out, with an eye toward filling in the gaps in your collection of colors.

5. Swap with friends. Don't expect to get a gem if you're not willing to part with some prize pieces, though.

6. Tell your friends and relatives who travel that you're collecting fabrics. They'll have an easy time of shopping for souvenirs for you, and you won't have to wonder what you're going to do with yet another set of scenic drink coasters.

7. Don't ever use the last scrap of anything. If you see that the quilt you've planned will clean out your entire stock of blues, shop for more blues before you start the quilt. Rather than depleting your collection, you will be adding variety to it.

In scrap quilts, as in all quilts, aim for the best; don't just "make do," make heirlooms!

ORGANIZING YOUR COLLECTION. There's not much point in collecting scraps if you don't use them. And I guarantee that you won't get around to using them if they are disorganized or inaccessible. Face it, which would you rather do: hop in the car and whiz over to the local quilt store to buy a couple quarter-yards or shimmy past the kids' bikes and the old patio furniture to the most remote corner of the garage, unearth the bottom carton, lug it into the house, dump its contents on the floor, and hope you can find that gem of a fabric that you thought you put in there—though it might be in that other box behind the rabbit hutch?

My personal experience testifies to the fact that a good scrap collection without a good organizing system is useless. I used to keep every snippet over one inch square. I'd toss these patches into three barrels: one for reds (and yellows and oranges); one for blues (and greens and purples); and one for blacks (and browns and beiges). Though I faithfully stashed my cutting scraps in the barrels, I seldom, if ever, pulled anything out of them. I couldn't remember if I put the rust in the barrel with the reds or with the browns. And I certainly did not want to go through two big barrels to find out. The barrels became so tightly packed and the contents so snarled that it was a major chore to rummage through them.

I still keep every tiny scrap. But now I keep them in small stacking bins—twelve of them—sorted by color. The bins are small enough that it is no trouble at all sifting through one—or several—for the perfect scrap. As my scrap collection grows, I'll simply add more bins and divide the contents of the fullest ones into subcolors. I still go to the local quilt store to fill out my own stash for a scrap quilt, but I also use pieces from my collection. And my quilts are richer and more meaningful to me for it.

I take my quiltmaking seriously. It is my business as well as my hobby. After years of "making do," this year my husband and I finished a basement sewing room, complete with a four foot by six foot walk-in closet fitted with shelves for my fabric and bins for my scraps. I've sorted yardage into prints and solids, folded each piece neatly, and arranged the collection in stacks by color. If I want to make a quilt from light blues, pinks, and yellows, I simply take the needed stacks from the closet, ignoring all the other colors. Nothing could be easier.

Of course, you will want to tailor your scrap-storage system to your own needs—to the space you have available, to the size of your scrap collection, and to your budget. If you live in a large metropolitan area, look for a store specializing in storage systems for a dazzling array of boxes, bins, shelves, and containers of all kinds. Many dime stores and discount stores also carry a selection of suitable organizers.

Here are some suggestions to fit scrap collections and budgets of all sizes:

STORAGE IDEAS: SMALL COLLECTIONS

1. Try a row of shoe boxes on a closet shelf. Be sure to label them clearly as to color. Don't stack them too high or you'll find it inconvenient to reach the top ones or dislodge the bottom ones.

2. Substitute clear plastic sweater boxes for

the shoe boxes. This is a bit more expensive, but it will be a joy to look at and easy to tell at a glance which box you need.

3. Choose opaque boxes in bright colors if your fabrics will be stored in a sunny room rather than in a closet. This will protect your fabrics from fading. Put your blue fabrics in a blue box, your pinks in a pink box, and so on, to make your scraps easy to find.

4. Arrange wicker baskets of scraps on your bookcase or worktable for an attractive, inexpensive solution to the scrap-storage problem.

STORAGE IDEAS: MODERATE COLLECTIONS

1. Stash your scraps in a spare dresser (or buy one just for this purpose). A dresser looks natural in a guest bedroom and is convenient. Make wooden dividers for large drawers, or cut down cardboard boxes to organize colors within each drawer.

2. Revive an old armoire, bookcase, china hutch, or chest, and fill every nook and cranny of it with scraps, neatly folded or in containers.

3. Buy a suitable number of bins or free-standing units with removable drawers, and set them up in your sewing room or closet.

STORAGE IDEAS: LARGE COLLECTIONS

1. Buy inexpensive steel canning shelves and fill them with shoe boxes or banker's boxes. More functional than attractive, this is ideal for closet or basement.

2. Bring your steel shelving out of the closet. Painted a pretty color, and filled with plastic boxes, this storage system looks good enough to take center stage in your sewing room.

3. Empty a seldom-used closet, and line it with built-in shelves or drawers or ready-made bins.

4. Build a wall of storage into your sewing room. Customize from countertops and cabinets designed for kitchens and bathrooms.

FABRIC PREPARATION. All scraps and yardage should be washed and dried to preshrink and test for colorfastness. As you won't want to be delayed by washing at the start of a new quilt project, make a point of laundering the materials as soon as you bring them home. Rinse each piece individually in warm water in the sink, squeezing until the water runs clear. When you are sure that the color is set, wash the fabrics in small batches in the washing machine. Use a little laundry detergent and a warm-wash, cool-rinse, permanent-press setting. Smooth out the wrinkles and fold the fabrics promptly, reserving ironing until you are about to cut out a quilt from the fabric.

For small scraps, especially narrow strips, the washing machine may tangle the pieces hopelessly. You may prefer to test these pieces for colorfastness, soak them in a sink full of warm water, and press them dry with a warm iron. Do be sure to prewash any scraps of unknown origin as well as new yardage.

PLANNING SCRAP QUILTS

Most often, scrap quilts are made from a large number of different fabrics in a wide range of colors. This may give the illusion of randomness, but actually, most quiltmakers use the same care in planning their scrap quilts that they use in their other quilts.

Scrap fabrics add interest and texture to an otherwise nondescript pattern, so scraps have long been associated with the simplest of patterns, such as Nine-Patch and Flying Geese. These are often developed in the multicolored arrangements that usually come to mind when we think of scrap quilts. However, scraps need not be reserved for only the most basic of patterns; used with care, scraps can enhance just about any quilt pattern.

SELECTING A PATTERN. One-patch quilts, allover patterns, and quilts of repeated blocks—set side by side, with sashes, or with alternate blocks—can all benefit from scraps. Nothing is out of bounds. In fact, just about every type of pattern is represented by the scrap quilts in this book: Stars at Sea (page 35) is a scrap variation of a very structured traditional pattern, Storm at Sea, which is usually pieced from a few related solids. Country Cousin (page 64) is a scrap version of a two-color counterchange pattern, similar to the traditional Robbing Peter to Pay Paul designs. Tennessee Waltz (page 60) is an allover pattern made up of two different pieced blocks alternating across the quilt surface. Pine Burr Beauty (page 36) is a traditional block with elaborate pieced

sashing. Bear's Paw (page 9) is a typical block-and-sash arrangement. Op-Ex (page 14) has blocks set side by side. April Wreath (page 57) is a central-medallion quilt in appliqué. Fantasy Vine (page 39) is a strippie quilt made in vertical rows instead of blocks. Arrowroot Medallion (page 37) has pieced-and-appliquéd blocks in a traditional arrangement with an appliquéd border of serpentine vines. Yank's Irish Chain (page 63) is a large bed quilt; Judy's Flower Patch (page 39) is a small wall hanging; Stacked Bricks (page 40) is an afghan or throw; Star of the Orient (page 57) can be a crib quilt or bed topper. Any type of quilt is within the realm of possibilities for scraps. You're not limited to the Grandmother's Flower Gardens and Double Wedding Rings usually associated with scraps. Any pattern you might choose for a nonscrap quilt—whether traditional or original—is fair game.

The key to a happy marriage of scraps and pattern lies in the range of scraps selected. Scraps in a carefully controlled color scheme can add just a subtle hint of textural interest to an already complex pattern, whereas a wide assortment of scraps can give needed punch to a simple design

KEEPING IN CONTROL. There are several ways of keeping a scrap quilt from getting out of control or looking haphazard, confusing, or overly complex: (1) You can limit your fabrics to a particular color scheme or mood as in Colorado Log Cabin on page 62. (2) You can rely on plenty of repetition in the shapes to supply the desired continuity. Stacked Bricks, page 40, or a one-patch like Grandmother's Flower Garden are good examples. (3) You can use one particular fabric throughout the quilt for a uniform background or setting or a recurring accent in the blocks. See Carpenter's Wheel on page 10. (4) You can focus on repeating blocks, making each from the same colors in the same positions, varying only the particular prints chosen as in Arrowroot Medallion, page 37. Or, (5) you can use careful sorting, good contrast, and well-balanced color distribution to minimize the individual blocks and patches in favor of a strong overall pattern like Stars at Sea on page 35.

If you have in mind some kind of plan, some notion of where you are headed, before you cut your first scrap, your quilt will surely shine with the care you put into it. Let's explore some ideas for making a scrap quilt with a difference.

CHOOSING A COLOR SCHEME. For nonscrap quilts and many scrap quilts as well, the color scheme is a very important design consideration. Drawing cues from the person or room for which the quilt is intended, available fabrics, the requirements of your chosen pattern, and your own personal tastes, you limit your colors to a well-coordinated few. That is, you decide on a color scheme. You may choose red, white, and blue; rose and green; brown, green, gold, and rust; or any other combination that suits you. It is easy to choose, by intuition, a few colors that look good together. You have surely seen enough color schemes to know a few combinations with which you feel comfortable; and working with just a few fabrics at a time, it is easy to experiment—to try new combinations—and to judge at a glance whether or not you like them.

Scrap quilts sometimes adhere to a color scheme, but just as often, they are made from a much broader assortment of fabrics than a typical color scheme encompasses. A scrap quilt might be made from red, orange, yellow, green, blue, and purple. That's not just a color scheme; that's the whole color wheel! The notion of trying every scrap with every other and making an intuitive decision in each case is overwhelming and irrelevant. How, then, do you limit your fabrics for a multicolored quilt so it looks "scrappy" and well-coordinated at the same time?

ESTABLISHING A MOOD. Set aside, for now, the idea of a color scheme, per se, and concentrate instead on a mood. The mood is the underlying harmony that makes a color scheme work.

Colors that share a feeling—whether it be bright and cheerful, somber and brooding, sweet and innocent, bold and imaginative, sophisticated and subtle, or earthy and handsome—go together no matter how many fabrics or hues you combine.

Let's choose, for example, a bright and cheerful mood and decide on an assortment of fabrics to express it. A good example is the Maltese Circles quilt on page 61. This quilt conveys a gaiety that is achieved through the use of clear, bright prints in a rainbow of colors. But the quilt doesn't contain every color in the book. It limits itself to clear, simple, primary and secondary colors in full strength and pastel tints. It has no complex, murky colors, no grayed tones, and no dark shades. It has no wine, rust, gold, avocado, navy, or plum; no mauve, celery, taupe, gray, or dusty rose; no brown; no black. There is nothing somber, sophisticated, subtle, daring, or handsome about it; just straightforward, unadulterated cheer.

Now let's examine other moods: Tennessee Waltz (page 60) is a good example of earthy and handsome. Sharp, crisp, clear-but-dark colors such as black, brown, rust, burgundy, teal blue, and forest green were selected. Simple brights, pastels, or murky shades (royal purple, pink, and khaki, for example) have no place here.

April Wreath (page 57) is sweet and innocent with aqua, coral, lilac, mint, yellow, and pink, the palette of the 1920s, '30s and '40s. Obviously, dark colors would not suit the mood of the other fabrics, and have been omitted. But the quilt still looks nice and scrappy with its limited palette.

The colors in Carpenter's Wheel (page 10) were chosen to give a subtle, sophisticated look—quiet shades of understated brown, blue, and gold, softened with a large dose of natural muslin. The colors are complex without being murky, all with rich golden overtones.

Arrowroot Medallion (page 37) is bold and imaginative, with complex shades, both bright and murky, and the kind of color tension, almost clashing, you find in an Amish quilt. Its hues don't fall into an easily categorized color scheme, but they do evoke a certain mood or feeling found in masterpiece quilts from the late 19th century.

I am sure that you can imagine other moods—bold and handsome, sweet and cheerful, bright and childlike—to name a few. Each mood or feeling has its own set of colors. With a little experience, you can readily match color to mood.

Perhaps you are more accustomed to thinking of harmonizing palettes in terms of seasons rather than moods. Think of the warm, dark colors of fall: rust, gold, brown, olive, burgundy, forest green, and teal blue. Or picture the soft, clear flower-bright colors of spring: daffodil, lilac, leafy green, rose and poppy red; the strong cool tones of winter: icy blue, steel gray, emerald green, taupe, royal purple, and magenta; or soft, cool hues of summer: powder pink, aqua, mint green, sky blue, and watermelon.

Or think of the colors associated with particular periods of decor: the turquoise, hot pink, red-orange, and gold of Danish modern; the rose, blue-gray, and celadon green of today's American country style; the turkey red and federal blue of colonial style; and so on. These are harmonizing palettes as well.

Or think of a palette associated with a favorite painter: Renoir's pink undertones, Gauguin's golden highlights, Picasso's blue period.

Keeping in mind the harmonies of moods, seasons, decorative styles, painters' palettes, or whatever relates to your personal experience, look at the scrap quilts in this book and in your other favorite sources. Examine the quilts that appeal most to you; identify their moods or palettes; decide what kinds of colors were included and—just as important—what colors were left out. Now assemble scrap fabrics from your own collection to fit in with the palette of a favorite quilt photo or idea. When you feel you understand color harmonies, you are ready to choose fabrics and colors for your own multi-colored scrap quilt.

DECIDING ON A RANGE OF COLORS. Choosing a mood or color scheme for your scrap quilt is just the beginning of your decision making. It is not enough to say that your quilt will be red and white, for there is a whole continuum of colors loosely called red and another set of colors that might be considered white. How far do you wish your colors to range? Will your reds include rust, wine, turkey red, rose, or scarlet? Will your whites extend into the beiges, creams, light browns, and light golds?

In deciding how far your colors will range, contrast is an important consideration. In a red-and-white quilt, such as Country Cousin (page 64), you can interpret your colors broadly without compromising contrast. A small or large color range becomes a matter of personal taste in cases like this. (Judge the different effects of broad or narrow color ranges in the two versions of Star Reel on page 59.)

However, if your quilt pattern calls for more subtle contrasts, as in Stars at Sea (page 35), you may need to limit the range of each color tightly. In this example, navy and baby blue must contrast in order for the pattern to develop. Therefore, the navy blues are decidedly dark, the baby blues are uniformly light, and medium blues were avoided altogether.

Decide how large a range of colors best suits your quilt, and list the acceptable shades. Remember that the cumulative effect will approximate the color in the middle of your range (lilacs, pinks, and peaches will have a pink look overall). Judge each fabric you are considering from your collection against this list.

PRESELECTING YOUR PALETTE. If there is any special "secret," any key to success with a scrap quilt, this is it: choose your palette of fabric and colors before you begin. Achieving your desired effect in a quilt is virtually automatic once your palette is selected. All you have to do is decide on a mood or color scheme; list colors that convey that mood or fit that color scheme; and assemble a collection of fabrics and scraps to match your listed colors. That's all there is to it. It is really very simple.

In sorting fabrics to determine whether they are suitable for your palette, judge the fabrics by the overall impression they create, usually governed by the background color of the print. Accent colors in a print need not worry you much, but do judge the way they affect the overall look of the fabric. Also, be sure to include a variety of visual textures: splashy prints, rhythmic figures of different scales, bold, blurred, dotty, airy, feathery, or swirly prints of every description.

The photos on page 16 show in detail the fabrics that make up the palettes of six of the quilts in this book. Compare the close-ups with the overall effect in the whole quilt photos. Study the variety and range of prints selected for each quilt.

As you gather fabrics for your quilt's palette, fan out your collected fabrics to get an overview of your palette. Use your intuition to cull anything that spoils the overall look. Notice any gaps or insufficiencies in your collection, and plan to fill in with new yardage as needed.

By limiting your prints and colors at the start, you can proceed almost randomly with the sewing and be confident of good results.

PLACING THE INDIVIDUAL FABRICS. Once you determine *whether* a scrap fits into your plan, you must decide *where* it fits. Looking at the scrap quilts pictured in this book, you will see that in order to develop the overall pattern of a quilt you need contrast. Most quiltmakers start with a block picture or some kind of plan for placing lights and darks or various specific colors in the quilt. For scrap quilts, you have a number of additional options for executing your plan in fabrics. (1) For every patch of the same color in the block you can use the same fabric. (2) Alternatively, you can choose several different prints of the same color. (3) You can make the various blocks all with the same color sense, or (4) you can make the same patches different colors in different blocks. (5) You can cut all your patches from scraps, or (6) you can use the same background fabric or accent color throughout. (7) You can make the blocks stand out, or (8) let the overall pattern of the quilt predominate.

Your choices should take into consideration the complexity of the pattern, the need for variation in a repetitive design, and the need for continuity in a potentially confusing one. Keep in mind, too, the overall effect of the quilt.

You will need to sort the fabrics from your palette according to your general plan. Make separate piles of lights and darks, or reds, whites, and blues, or whatever categories fit your pattern. Beyond this initial sorting, the placement of patches can be virtually random. As you sew, you will want to avoid placing prints that are identical or too similar next to each other. You may want to pay some attention to the scales and textures of neighboring prints, and avoid clumping all the little spriggy prints in one place and the splashy prints somewhere else. But there is no need to agonize over the exact placement of each individual patch. You can make the decisions easily, as you sew. Just pick up the next two patches to be sewn together; if you feel the contrast isn't right, simply set aside one patch and see if the next patch in the pile makes a more suitable partner. Anyone can do it. One little "mistake" will be lost in the whole quilt. It is sufficient to sort your fabrics according to a general placement plan, and join patches pretty much randomly, with a few combinations rejected by a quick, intuitive reaction.

If your plan calls for blocks of a few coordinated fabrics, with the combinations changing from block to block, you will want to plan the placement of each fabric in the same way you would plan a quilt from just a few fabrics. For this kind of quilt, you need to remember to contrast the colors, scales, and visual textures of adjacent patches. (This can be done in a leisurely fashion—select fabrics, cut, and sew a single block at a time.) Of course, even here the placement of any one piece will not make or break your quilt, as it might if the block were to be repeated in the same fabrics many times.

Whether your quilt has a block focus or a predominating overall design, you will want to distribute the colors evenly across the surface of the quilt. Balanced color will lead the eye across the quilt, whereas poorly distributed color—with all the red clumped in one corner, for example—will draw the eye to the problem area. Be especially careful to place in a balanced fashion those individual fabrics that stand out in some way. This is easily accomplished if you cut out all of the patches before sewing any and if you make all of the blocks before joining any into rows. Once the blocks are made, you can stack them in order of similarity and "deal" them (like playing cards) into piles, one for each row. Then all you have to do is lay out the rows and switch a few blocks here and there to achieve good color balance.

Remember that the placement of individual patches is not as important as the overall idea, the initial selection of a palette, and the careful sorting into placement categories. Part of the appeal of scrap quilts lies in their apparent "randomness." It is okay for some small areas in the quilt to demand more attention than others. It is all right for two red prints to touch one another. It is fine for two calicoes of similar scales to lie side by side. Small things that might be viewed as mistakes in other quilts only add to the character of a scrap quilt. The little eccentricities are charming as long as your basic idea prevails and the overall effect is unspoiled.

HOW TO MAKE A QUILT

SCRAP QUILTS PATTERNS. We give seam lines (dashed) as well as cutting lines (solid) for the full-sized pieced patterns in *SCRAP QUILTS.* The seam allowances are ¼" for all pieced patterns, and the points are trimmed. Pretrimming reduces bulk in the seams and also provides clues for exact alignment of patches for machine sewing. These trims are positioned to make the seam lines of adjoining patches fall into place for stitching when the cut edges and the trimmed points are aligned.

Very large pieces such as alternate blocks or setting triangles are shown in miniature with dimensions. Use graph paper to rule these patterns in the measurements given or measure and mark them directly onto the fabric if you can duplicate the proper angles with a carpenter's square, right triangle, or similar tool. The dimensions shown do *not* include seam allowances. Be sure to add them when you mark and cut your fabric.

Seam allowances (plus two inches extra length for insurance) are included in the dimensions listed for borders and other long strips in the "Materials Needed" box for each pattern.

No turn-under allowances are given for the appliqué patterns. You will add the ³⁄₁₆" by eye when cutting.

If we give just half of the pattern piece, the center line is indicated with a dotted line. When making the template, simply trace around the pattern, flip the tracing over, and align the dotted center lines. Trace around the pattern again to complete the template for the whole patch.

When our quilt specifications call for a pattern letter followed by an "r," you will need to reverse the pattern. That is, if the instructions call for 36 A and 36 Ar, mark the first 36 patches, then turn the template over to mark the remaining 36.

MAKING TEMPLATES. Carefully trace pattern pieces directly onto clear template plastic, or trace on paper and glue the tracing to sandpaper, plastic, or cardboard. Cut out accurately to make template. See specific instructions for the sewing method of your choice to determine whether to trace seam lines or cutting lines when making templates.

Make a sample block to test the accuracy with which you have made templates before cutting out the whole quilt.

FABRIC PREPARATION. Always wash and iron fabrics before cutting them into patches. The cotton fabrics that most quiltmakers use are likely to shrink, and their colors may run. Rinse dark colors separately to check for excess dye. If the color bleeds, continue rinsing until the water runs clear.

Plan to measure, mark, and cut border strips first and larger patches before smaller ones from the same fabric. Arrange patches with cutting lines of neighboring patches close or touching for best use of fabric.

GRAIN LINE. When marking and cutting

patches, consider the grain line of the fabric. Generally, one or more straight sides of the patch should follow the lengthwise or crosswise grain. This is especially true of sides that will be on the outside edges of the quilt block. Wherever possible, we indicate lengthwise or crosswise grain with an arrow on the pattern piece.

HAND PIECING. Patches for hand piecing require precisely marked seam lines, but marked cutting lines are optional. Most hand piecers prefer a template that does not include a seam allowance.

To mark the patches, place the template *face down* on *wrong* side of fabric and draw around it accurately with a pencil. Leave just enough space between patches to add ¼″ seam allowances when cutting.

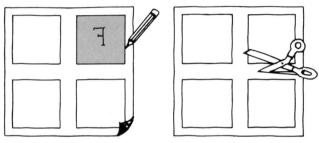

After marking the patches, cut outward from the seam line about ¼″, measuring the distance by eye. The pieces will be joined right sides together, so the marked seam line on the wrong side of the fabric is visible on both sides of the patchwork when sewing. Sew the seam right through the penciled lines, so that your patchwork will fit perfectly. Join the patches with a short running stitch, using a single thread. Begin and end each seam at seam line (not at edge of fabric) with two or three backstitches to secure seam.

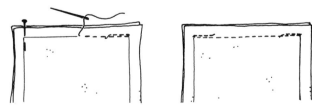

Use a dark-colored thread with dark fabrics and a light-colored thread with light ones. When you are sewing a dark patch to a light one, match the thread to the fabric toward which you will be pressing the seam allowances (usually the dark color). A short needle (such as size 7 or 8 between) will work best.

MACHINE PIECING. Many machine patchworkers prefer to include the seam allowances in the

template and mark the cutting line instead of the sewing line. The reason for this is that accurate cutting is very important in machine piecing.

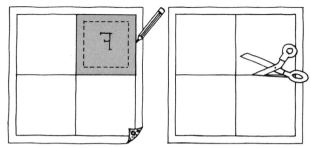

When sewing patches together on the machine, align the cut edges with the edge of the presser foot if the foot is ¼″ wide. If not, place a

piece of masking tape on the throat plate of the machine ¼″ away from the needle to guide you in making precise ¼″ seams. Sew all the way to the cut edge unless you are inserting a patch into an angle. For machine piecing you may want to match thread color to the patches (even using a different color for top and bobbin threads). However, if you are using very many colors, you may prefer to use a single thread color such as beige that won't show much on any of the fabrics.

HAND APPLIQUÉ. Templates for hand appliqué do not include turn-under allowances. To mark patches for hand appliqué, place template *face up* on the right side of the fabric and draw around it lightly with a pencil.

Turn under ³⁄₁₆″ allowance on each appliqué, and baste in place. (Do not turn under edges that will be tucked under other appliqués.) Clip well into the allowance of inward curves to make pieces lie flat.

If background block is a light color, lay it over pattern in the book, matching centers, to see placement for appliqués. Lightly mark major shapes with a pencil, or simply pin appliqués into position. If you cannot see through the background block, finger-crease the block in half lengthwise, crosswise, and diagonally to form guidelines for placement of appliqués.

Pin or baste appliqué patches onto the background fabric, tucking raw edges under adjacent appliqués as needed. Appliqué with an invisible slip stitch or hemming stitch in a thread color that matches the patch, not the background. Remove basting.

To facilitate the quilting later and to prevent show-through after applying each patch, carefully

 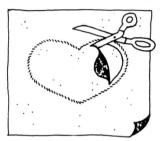

cut away background fabric from behind appliqués using sharp scissors and trimming to within 3⁄16″ of seam line. Reinforce seams with a couple of stitches if it is necessary to cut across seam lines when trimming.

PRESSING. Press all seams to one side (not open), usually toward the darker fabric. Quilt blocks should be pressed flat with no puckers, and they should be square and measure exactly the same size as the other blocks. If any quilt block has problems, remove a few stitches to ease away puckers. All parts of the quilt top—blocks, sashing, and borders—should be well pressed and accurately measured.

SETTING BLOCKS TOGETHER. For adjacent or alternate blocks, join the blocks for the first row with 1⁄4″ seams. Then join all blocks in the second row, and so on, until all rows are completed. Press all seams in the odd-numbered rows in one direction and all seams in the even-numbered rows in the opposite direction. When all rows are completed, pin two rows together so that seam lines match perfectly. Join rows together in groups of two, then four, and so on, until top is completed. Press all seams in one direction, either up or down. When setting blocks and rows together, be careful to avoid stretching them. If sashing strips will be used, sew short sashing strips between the blocks in a row, pressing all seams either toward or away from the sashing

strips. Sew sashing strips between rows of blocks, as well.

ADDING MITERED BORDERS. Measure the quilt top, being careful not to stretch it. (You'll get a more accurate measurement if you measure in a few different places, across the midsection of the quilt rather than along the edge.) Fold the quilt in half to find the center, and put a pin along the edge of the quilt top at the center of each side. Similarly fold the border strips to find their centers, marking these with pins. Measure the border strip (from the center out in both directions), and mark each end to correspond to the measurement for your quilt top. (Recall that the dimensions for borders listed in this book include two inches extra length for insurance). Now, center a border strip on each side of the quilt top to extend equally at each end. Match marks on borders to ends of quilt top. Pin and sew strips in 1⁄4″ seams, beginning and ending the seam at the seam line, not at outer edge of fabric. At one corner (on wrong side), smooth one border over an adjacent one and draw a diagonal line from inner seam line to the point where outer edges of two borders cross. Reverse the two borders (bottom one is now on top), and again draw a diagonal line from inner seam line to point where outer edges cross. Match the two pencil lines (fabrics right sides together), and sew through them. Cut away excess, and press seam. Repeat at other three corners of quilt.

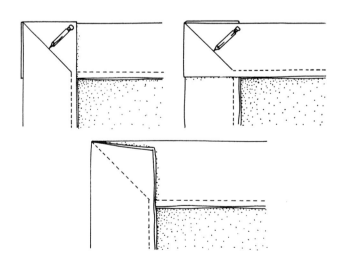

MARKING FOR QUILTING. Place quilting pattern under quilt top. Mark design on quilt top very lightly with a pencil. Place the design over a light source to mark dark-colored fabrics, using a chalk pencil. Water-soluble pens are also available, but be sure to test for removability on a scrap before marking the whole quilt.

Some of the quilting may be done without marking the top at all. Outline quilting (¼" from seam around patches) or quilting "in the ditch" (right next to the seam on the side without the seam allowances) can be done "by eye." Other straight lines may also be "marked" as you quilt by using a piece of masking tape, which is pulled away after a line is quilted along its edge.

LINING. Make a quilt lining that is about 2" larger on each side than the quilt top. Some quilts are small enough to require a single piece for lining, but usually two or three lengths of the yard goods must be seamed together. Remove selvedges from these lengths of fabric to avoid puckers; press seams to one side to prevent the batting from bearding through between stitches.

Place the lining, wrong side up, on a flat surface. Spread the quilt batt over the lining, making sure that both stay smooth and even. Then place the quilt top, right side up, on top of the batting. Pin the three layers as necessary to hold them together while basting. Beginning in the center, baste all layers together in an "X," then in rows four to six inches apart. Also baste around edges. Now you are ready to quilt or tie.

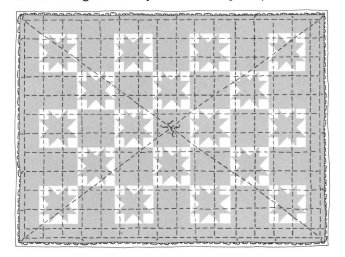

QUILTING. Some quilters use a large frame; others use a quilting hoop; and some just quilt in their laps with no frame at all. Quilting is done in a short running stitch with a single strand of thread that goes through all three layers. Use a short needle (8 or 9 between) with about 18" of thread. Make a small knot in the thread, and take a first long stitch (about 1") through top and batting only, coming up where the quilting will begin. Tug on the thread to pull the knotted end between the layers. Take straight, even stitches that are the same size on the top and lining sides of the quilt. For tiny stitches, push the needle with a thimble on your middle finger, and guide the fabric in front

of the needle with the thumb of your hand above the quilt and thumb and index finger of your hand below the quilt. To end a line of quilting, take a tiny backstitch, and then make another inch-long stitch through the top and batting only. Clip thread at surface of quilt, and let the "tail" slip back into the batting. Remove basting stitches when you finish quilting.

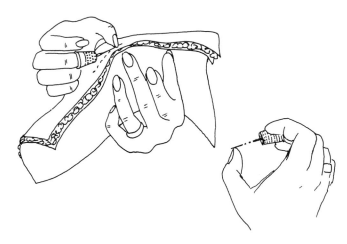

TYING. This is a quick alternative to quilting. Line quilt top as described above, basting or not, as desired. To mark placement for ties, insert pins through all layers (top, batting, and lining) at each block center and corner, or at other logical places related to the design. Also pin around borders. Space pins not more than 6" apart. Thread a sharp, large-eyed needle with about two yards of three-ply acrylic baby yarn or fingering yarn, and pull it up doubled. Don't knot it. Insert needle beside a pin marking placement for a tie, from either top or lining side (whichever side you want to have tails of knots). Remove pin. Take a stitch about ¼" long through all layers, and bring needle back up near where it entered. Pull up yarn, leaving a 2" tail for a square knot. Tie knot and trim ends. Repeat at each pin. Remove basting, if any.

BINDING AND FINISHING. Trim quilt batt and lining even with quilt top. Leaving about 2" extra at each end, place a 1½" binding strip on one edge of quilt top, right sides together. Sew through all layers (binding, quilt top, batting, lining) with a ¼" seam, beginning and ending at

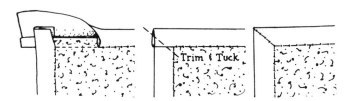

Trim & Tuck

seam line. Repeat for other three sides of quilt. Fold binding to the back, tucking under ¼", and blindstitch it down along seam line. At corners, trim, tuck in ends, and stitch.

Be sure to rinse out any quilt marking that still shows. A nice finishing touch is to embroider your name, city, and date on the back of your quilt.

SPECIAL TIPS FOR SCRAP QUILTS. Preselect your palette; then sort the fabrics you have gathered into piles, keeping together all the fabrics that will be used interchangeably. Count the number of fabrics in each pile. Your pattern will tell you how many patches of each type you'll need for the whole quilt. Divide the total number needed of one patch by the number of fabrics in the appropriate pile to find out how many patches of that type to cut from each fabric. For example, Maltese Circles (page 61) requires bright and pastel scraps, so sort your selected fabrics into these two categories. Count the fabrics in the brights pile. Suppose you count 42 brights. This pattern calls for 252 C's in bright scraps. Divide 252 by 42 and you'll learn you need to cut six C's from each fabric in the brights pile. Determine the number to cut of other patches in the same way.

For allover scrap patterns (such as Country Cousin, page 64), you will achieve a more even distribution of colors and fabrics if you cut out the entire quilt before piecing any of it and if you sew all the blocks before joining them into rows.

However, if you are impatient to see what your quilt will look like, you can cut out just enough to make a small section of the quilt. Use each fabric for just one patch in the segment and be sure to include the full range of colors to be used in the quilt. This way, you can judge the effect without delay, and you can incorporate this segment into the rest of the quilt later without spoiling the color balance.

For quilts whose individual blocks stand out more than the overall pattern, such as Pine Burr Beauty (page 36), you don't need to count fabrics and divide into the total number needed; and you don't need to cut out the whole quilt before beginning the piecing. It is still a good idea to preselect your palette. From the gathered fabrics, choose fabrics for a single block at a time. Sew one block before cutting the next. When you have made all of the blocks, join them into rows.

For the best color balance, sort the completed blocks in order of similarity: first the blocks with a certain red print, then blocks with a similar red print, followed by rust prints, then brown prints, and so on. Stack the blocks into piles, one for each row of the quilt. Then lay out the rows on the floor, rearranging the order of blocks in a row to get the best effect. Stand back and judge the overall impression. Switch blocks here and there, if necessary. Pick up the blocks in order, labeling the top block of each row, so you can keep them in order as you sew them into rows.

QUICK CUTTING WITHOUT MARKING. You can cut 400-800 pieces per hour, from scraps or collected yardage, without any marking whatsoever. Simply make a template with seam allowances already added. Make it on graph paper or one of the flexible template plastics. Prewash and press scraps or yardage, and smooth out a single layer of the first fabric on the ironing board. Place a second fabric on top of the first, aligning lengthwise grains, and press. Continue layering and pressing from four to eight fabrics. Put the smaller scraps on top and align everything on the bottom and right ends so that when you cut starting at that corner, you won't run off the edge of any of the fabrics. Where possible, put on the top layer any fabrics with prints that must be cut perfectly on grain (such as microdots or stripes). Pin the pattern piece to the top fabric or simply hold it in place with your fingers as you cut through all layers with a good, sharp pair of scissors. If you feel the scissors pulling and dragging too much, you are trying to cut too many layers for the quality and sharpness of your shears. Holding the pattern piece in place with your fingers takes a little practice, but as you gain experience, you'll find that you can be every bit as accurate with this method as with any slower method.

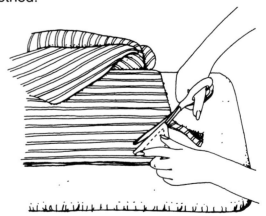

QUILT PATTERNS

This section features patterns for the 19 quilts shown in color within it, as well as for the quilt shown on page 9 (Plate I). These patterns include yardage figures, cutting requirements, complete instructions, and diagrams plus quilting patterns where applicable. Pattern pieces have seam lines (dashed) as well as cutting lines (solid). Grain lines (lengthwise or crosswise) are shown with an arrow in each pattern piece. Quilting patterns are shown with dashed lines. Dotted lines indicate the fold where half patterns are given due to space limitations. Complete the other half of the pattern when you make templates for cutting patches. Occasionally a small pattern piece overlaps a larger one on the page. Be sure to include the entire portion covered by the small patch when you make the template for the larger pattern piece. Border dimensions include ¼″ seam allowances and two inches extra length for insurance. Trim them after you have made the quilt top and checked its measurements for accuracy. Helpful hints are included for many patterns; you may want to read all of these even if you don't plan to make the quilts. Read "How to Make a Quilt" on pages 24-28 for complete descriptions of the techniques and procedures used in making these quilts.

BEAR'S PAW

The blue sashing and borders give this antique quilt a cheerful unity. The design (and the fact that the quilt takes over 1000 of the small triangles) make this a good quilt to put together in odd moments—choosing fabrics, cutting, then sewing a single block at a time rather than cutting the whole quilt at once and piecing it assembly-line style. Bear's Paw is shown in color on page 9.

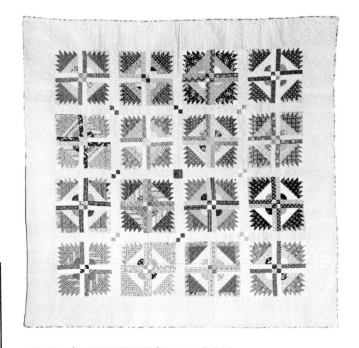

MATERIALS NEEDED

Block Size: 15″. Quilt Size: 79½″ x 79½″.
2½ yds. Blue Print: 4 borders 6½″ x 82″, 24 G.
¾ yd. Brown Print: binding 1½″ x 9½ yds.
6 yds. or Scraps in Various Prints:
      164 A, 64 B, 64 C, 64 D, 1024 E,
      128 F.
4¾ yds. Lining. 83½″ x 83½″ Batting.

1. Referring to block and unit drawings and piecing diagrams, make 16 blocks and 9 Unit 1's, each colored differently.

2. Join 4 blocks alternately with 3 G's to make a block row. Make 4 block rows.

3. Join 4 G's alternately with 3 Unit 1's to make a sash row. Make 3 sash rows.

4. Join block and sash rows, alternating types.

5. Add borders, mitering corners and trimming excess from seam allowances.

6. Mark and quilt feathers, cables, or the motif of your choice in the borders. Quilt "in the ditch" around E's. Outline quilt ¼″ from seam line around other patches. Bind to finish.

BLOCK

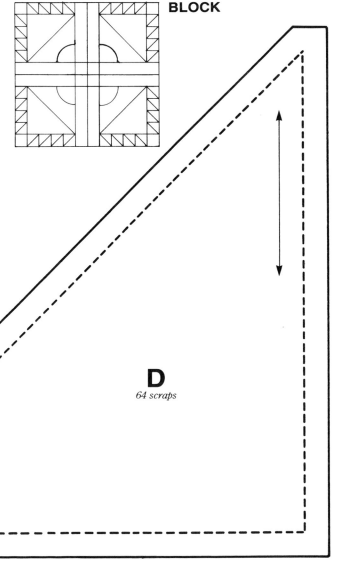

D
64 scraps

BLOCK PIECING

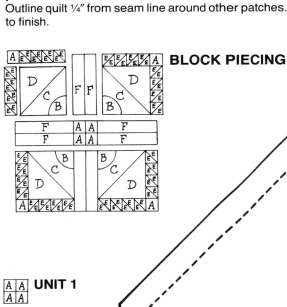

UNIT 1

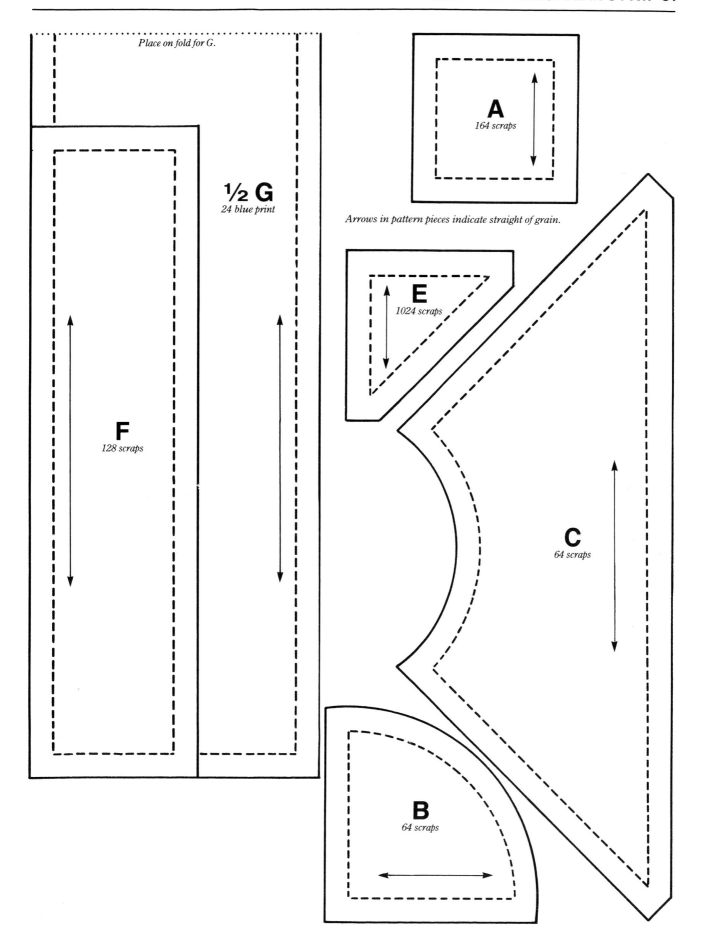

Place on fold for G.

½ G
24 blue print

F
128 scraps

A
164 scraps

Arrows in pattern pieces indicate straight of grain.

E
1024 scraps

C
64 scraps

B
64 scraps

LEMOYNE STAR

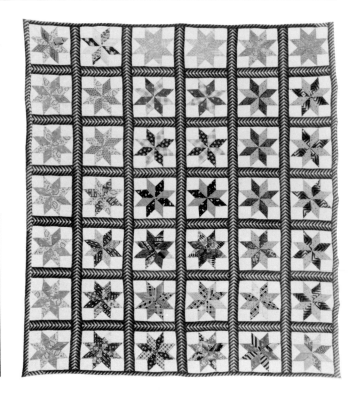

This pattern has long been a favorite for Scrap Quilt makers. Notice how stripes and plaids were combined with prints in a carefully planned color scheme for a very handsome antique quilt, shown in color on page 34.

MATERIALS NEEDED

Block Size: 10¼″. Quilt Size: 78″ x 90¾″.
2¾ yds. Blue Stripe: 2 borders 2½″ x 93¼″, 2 borders 2½″ x 80½″, 5 strips 3″ x 89¼″, 36 B.
3 yds. Muslin: binding 1½″ x 10 yds., 168 D, 168 K.
3¼ yds. or Scraps in Various Dark Prints: 336 A.
5⅝ yds. Lining. 82″ x 94¾″ Batting.

1. Note that pattern piece D is on page 94 and K is on page 95. Referring to block drawing and piecing diagram, make 42 blocks, each using a different pair of scrap prints.
2. Join 7 blocks alternately with 6 B's to make a vertical row. Make 6 vertical rows.
3. Sew the six vertical rows alternately with the five 89¼″ strips. (Note that strip and border measurements include seam allowances and 2″ extra length for insurance. Measure your pieced rows, and trim strips to fit.)
4. Add borders. Miter corners, trimming excess from seam allowances.
5. Outline quilt the patches. Quilt sashes, borders, and background as desired. Bind to finish.

BLOCK

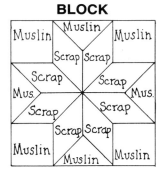

BLOCK PIECING

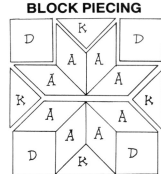

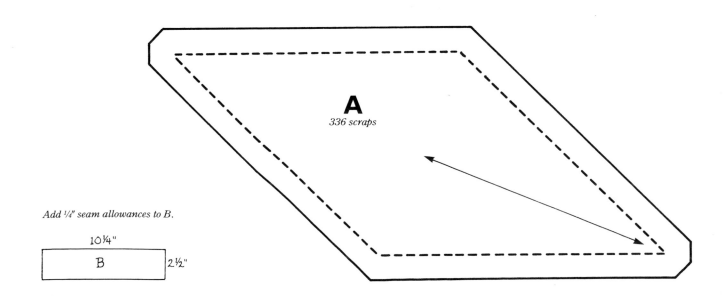

A
336 scraps

Add ¼″ seam allowances to B.

10¼″
B
2½″

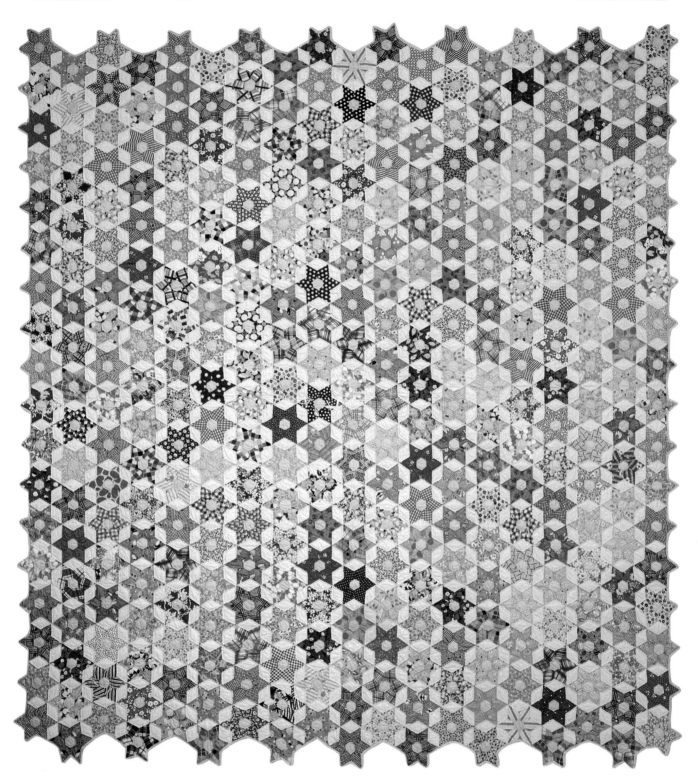

PLATE XVI: Texas Star, 79¾″ x 88″, circa 1940, from the collection of Bonnie Leman. This quilt is made from an assortment of 1930s prints, some of them salvaged from feed sacks. The maker apparently was not able to be selective in the prints chosen for this quilt, since she (or he) mixed bold plaids, checks, and strongly colored prints randomly with softer, more delicate pastels. In an examination of this quilt, star by star, some colors and prints can be found that are far from ideal—the few black prints being the most notable examples. Yet the overall effect is pleasing. The quilt succeeds because the prints are generally compatible, and their many colors add up to a richness of texture that overcomes the imperfections. Pattern on page 48.

PLATE XVII: Lemoyne Star, 90″ x 80″, circa 1845, from the collection of Thos. K. Woodard: American Antiques & Quilts. Chevron sashes dart across a field of stars to keep the eye from resting in any one spot. If you look carefully at some of the blocks, you can see the same blue chevron fabric in some of the diamonds—but it is sometimes pieced, which indicates that the maker was truly using even her smallest scraps. Although most of the blocks have brown fabric, the real unifying design factor is the sashing. (Photo courtesy E. P. Dutton, Inc.)

PLATE XVIII: Stars at Sea, 72″ x 90″, a slight variation of a traditional Storm at Sea (the four-patch block centers make the difference). Pieced by Ann Elliott; quilted by Jeanette Goodrich. Within the planned dark and light blue scheme, prints are placed randomly in blocks so that the overall pattern in the quilt will be more important than the individual blocks. About 100 different navy blues and 100 different light blues were used. As the contrast between the light and dark blues is important, the colors do not range very far. Pattern is on page 41.

PLATE XIX: Pine Burr Beauty, 76″ x 97″, traditional Pine Burr block combined with a set adapted from New York Beauty. Pieced by Brenda Bain; quilted by Judy Leo. About 50 different fabrics in browns, rusts, greens, and golds are arranged in blocks—each with a different color sense. Solids are the same throughout the quilt for unity. Pattern is on page 44.

PLATE XX: Arrowroot Medallion, 63″ x 63″, a traditional Arrowroot block with framing strips and appliqué border designed by Judy Martin. Pieced and appliquéd by Shirley Wegert; quilted by Geri Waechter. Each of the blocks uses different fabrics in the same basic placement.

About 18 different red prints range from rose and coral to rust and maroon. The 9 golds and 25 greens have a narrower range. Colors clash a bit to keep the quilt lively, and the background is a very light willow green for a subtle difference. Pattern is on page 65.

PLATE XXI: Judy's Flower Patch, 90″ x 94″. Ruby McKim's Modernistic Tulip provided the inspiration for this original design by Judy Martin. Pieced by Shirley Wegert; quilted by Phyllis Street. About 11 different green prints, 11 dark pinks and purples, 11 light pinks and purples, 29 light blues, pinks, and greens, and 27 medium blues and purples were used. Pink or purple fabrics were paired in close shades for a flower and each combination was repeated several times to make the 43 quilt blocks. Pattern is on page 52.

PLATE XXII: Judy's Flower Patch (Small), ▶
23″ x 32″, designed and pieced by Judy Martin;
quilted by Louise O. Townsend. This wall quilt
makes a lovely companion piece to the bed
quilt in Plate XXI. Nine different green prints
plus 12 lights and 12 pinks provide the scrap
interest in this small quilt. Pattern is on page
51.

▼ **PLATE XXIII:** Fantasy Vine, 49″ x 57″,
original design by Judy Martin. Pieced by
Louise O. Townsend; quilted by Mina Slade.
About 30 different soft greens and 60 bright
prints were used. Pattern is on page 49.

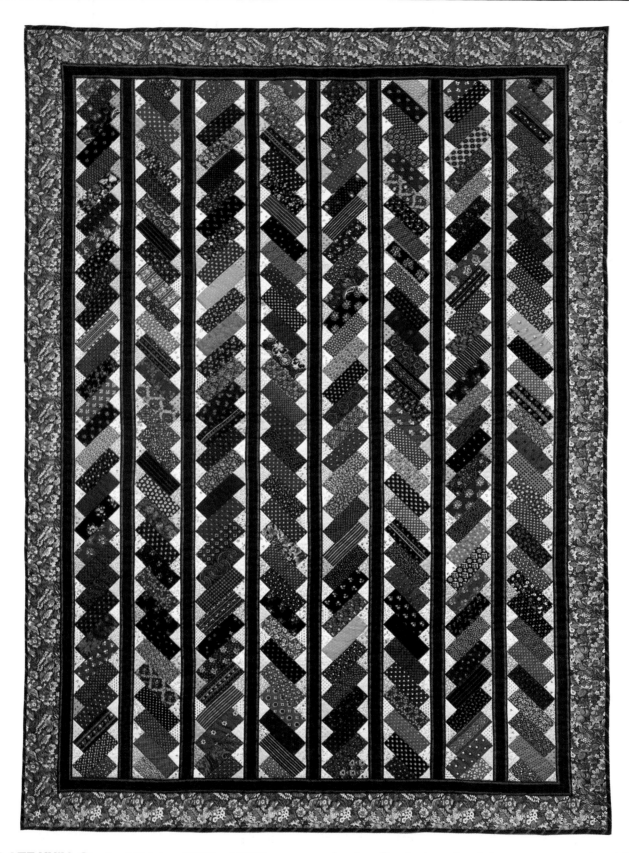

PLATE XXIV: Stacked Bricks, 52½″ x 72½″, variation of a traditional design. Pieced by Marla Stefanelli; quilted by Louise Morrison. "Bricks" range from gold to black in all the clear, dark shades. Background patches are scraps in white to light beige or light gold prints. Almost 250 different dark prints were used, along with about 60 light prints. Pattern is on page 55.

STARS AT SEA

This pattern is a variation of the old favorite, Storm at Sea, which is usually executed in just three fabrics. However, scraps that are carefully sorted into light and dark blues bring out the wavy pattern perfectly, as well as adding surface interest that invites close inspection. The quilt is shown in color on page 35.

MATERIALS NEEDED

Block Size: 9". Quilt Size: 72" x 90".
2¾ yds. White Solid: 252 B, 220 D, 220 Dr, 48 G.
2¼ yds. or Scraps in Various Navy Prints: 126 A, 110 E, 192 F.
2¼ yds. or Scraps in Various Medium Blue Prints: 126 A, 252 C.
2⅜ yds. Navy Stripe: 2 borders 2" x 83½", 2 borders 2" x 65½"
2⅝ yds. Medium Blue Print: 2 borders 5" x 92½", 2 borders 5" x 72½".
¾ yd. Navy Print: binding 1½" x 9½ yds.
5⅜ yds. Lining. 76" x 94" Batting.

1. Referring to block and unit drawings and piecing diagrams, make 48 blocks, 15 Unit 1's and 14 Unit 2's.
2. Join six blocks to make a row, being careful to position each block with the same side up (to match the block drawing). Make eight rows like this. Join rows.
3. Join eight Unit 1's alternately with eight Unit 2's. Sew to right side of quilt. Join the remaining seven Unit 1's alternately with six Unit 2's. Sew to bottom of quilt.
4. Sew a short navy stripe border to a short medium blue border, matching centers. Sew to top of quilt. Repeat for bottom of quilt. Similarly sew a long navy border to a long medium blue border and sew to side of quilt, matching centers. Repeat for other side. Miter corners, trimming excess from seam allowances.
5. Mark cable quilting in medium blue borders, with ends of motif aligning with diamond points. The last motif on each end of each border aligns with the seam between navy and medium blue border strips. Mark four corner motifs. Quilt as marked. Outline quilt or quilt "in the ditch" between patches. Bind in navy print to finish.

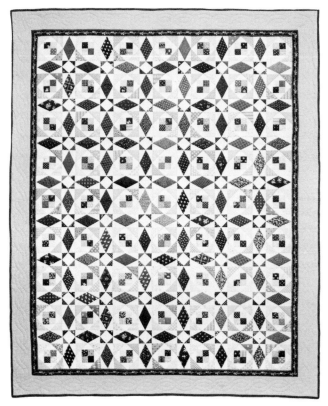

BLOCK
BLOCK PIECING

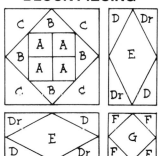

UNIT 1
UNIT 1 PIECING

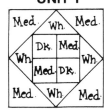
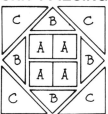

UNIT 2
UNIT 2 PIECING

Hints and Helps: To accentuate the diagonal movement in the quilt, place all four-patches with navy squares in the same position.

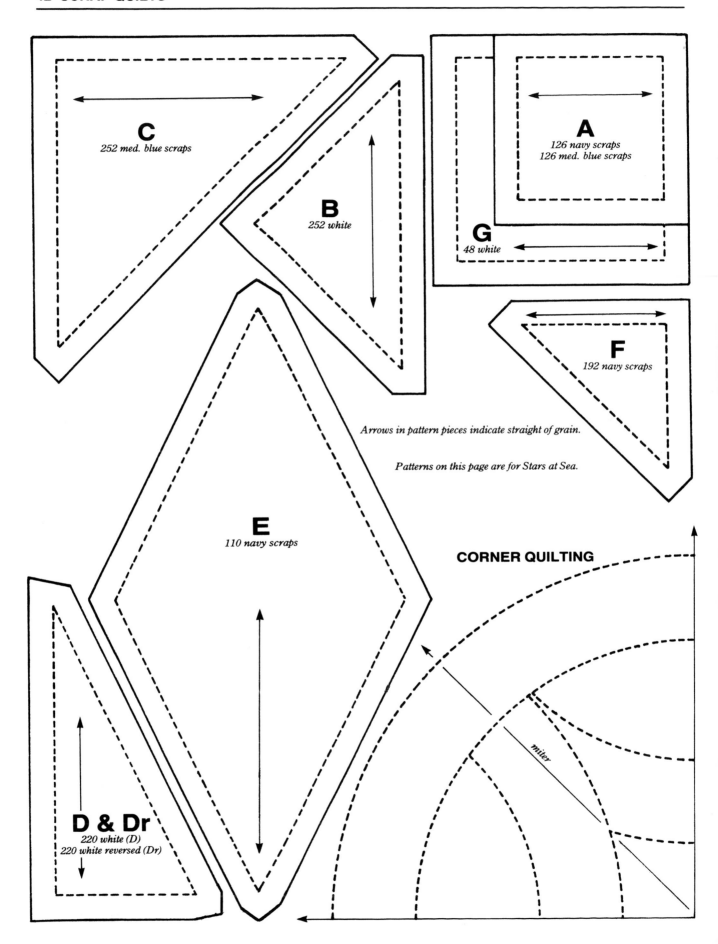

C
252 med. blue scraps

B
252 white

A
126 navy scraps
126 med. blue scraps

G
48 white

F
192 navy scraps

E
110 navy scraps

Arrows in pattern pieces indicate straight of grain.

Patterns on this page are for Stars at Sea.

CORNER QUILTING

miter

D & Dr
220 white (D)
220 white reversed (Dr)

STARS AT SEA BORDER QUILTING

Arrows in pattern pieces indicate straight of grain.

D and E are for Pine Burr Beauty, on next page.

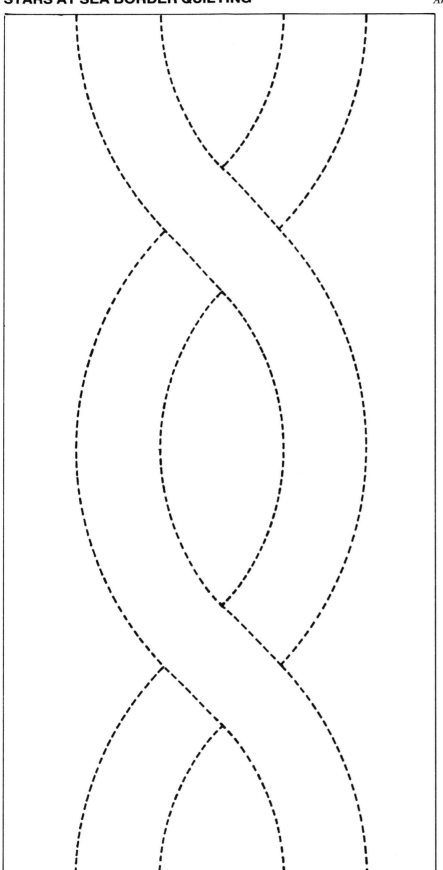

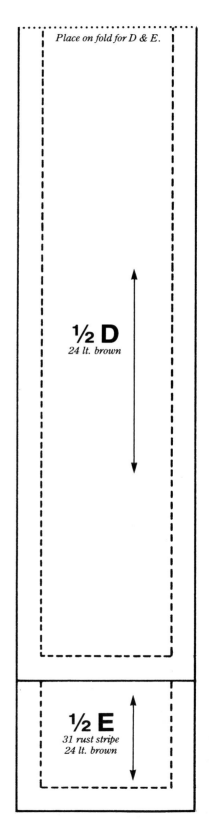

Place on fold for D & E.

½ D
24 lt. brown

½ E
31 rust stripe
24 lt. brown

PINE BURR BEAUTY

This is an easy quilt to piece, though its large number of pieces will require patience. You'll need to sew the triangles accurately to assure good crisp points. The color scheme (see photo on page 36) brings to mind pine trees and rugged mountains, but the pattern would be equally pretty in another color scheme of your choice.

MATERIALS NEEDED

Block Size: 15¾". Quilt Size: 76" x 97".

2⅜ yds. **Green Solid:** binding 1½" x 10¼ yds., 434 A.

2¾ yds. **Cream Solid:** 372 A, 48 C, 48 Cr, 62 F, 62 Fr, 80 H.

2¾ yds. **Light Brown Solid:** 2 borders 1⅞" x 94½", 2 borders 1⅞" x 73½", 24 D, 24 E.

½ yd. **Rust Print:** 80 G, 20 I.

2⅞ yds. **Rust Stripe:** 2 borders 3" x 99½", 2 borders 3" x 78½", 31 E.

2⅝ yds. **or Scraps in Various Green, Gold, Rust, and Brown Prints:** 432 A, 48 B.

5¾ yds. **Lining. 80" x 101" Batting.**

1. Referring to block and unit drawings and piecing diagrams, make 12 blocks, 31 Unit 1's, and 20 Unit 2's.

2. Join four Unit 2's alternately with three Unit 1's to make a sash row. Make five sash rows. Join four Unit 1's alternately with three blocks to make a block row. Join block and sash rows, alternating types.

3. Sew a short light brown border strip to a short rust stripe border strip, matching centers. Sew to top of quilt, again matching centers. Similarly sew a long light brown border to a long rust stripe border, and sew to side of quilt, matching centers. Repeat for other side of quilt. Miter corners, trimming excess from seam allowances.

4. Outline quilt or quilt "in the ditch" around patches and along border seam lines. Bind in green to finish.

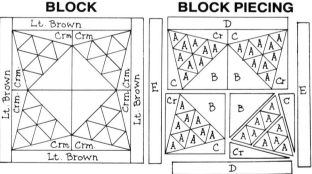

BLOCK   **BLOCK PIECING**

Hints and Helps: These blocks make great pick-up work to do at a leisurely pace. Because each block uses a different batch of coordinated prints, you can cut out just enough patches for a single block and sew them together before cutting out the next block. On the other hand, the sashes (Unit 1's) are perfect for fast assembly-line sewing. Switch from blocks to sashes to take advantage of your mood.

If you are careful to keep the green solid and cream so that the straight of grain is along the edge of dogtooth strip, you will not have to contend with stretchy bias when you sew the dogtooth strips to the rust stripe E or the Unit 1's to Unit 2's and blocks.

UNIT 1   **UNIT 2**

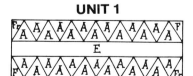

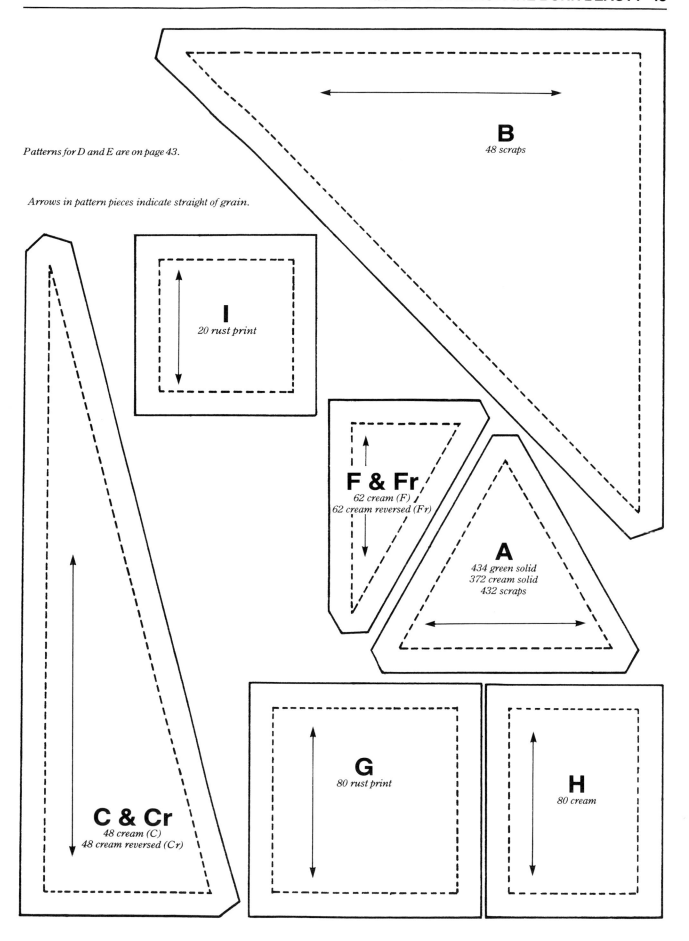

Patterns for D and E are on page 43.

Arrows in pattern pieces indicate straight of grain.

B
48 scraps

I
20 rust print

F & Fr
62 cream (F)
62 cream reversed (Fr)

A
434 green solid
372 cream solid
432 scraps

C & Cr
48 cream (C)
48 cream reversed (Cr)

G
80 rust print

H
80 cream

APRIL WREATH

This pretty wreath is perfect for using the tiniest scraps in an assortment of pastels. See the quilt in color on page 57.

MATERIALS NEEDED

Block Size: 20". Quilt Size: 36" x 36".

⅝ yd.	**White Solid:**	1 L.
1 yd.	**Aqua Stripe:**	12 M.
1⅛ yds.	**Coral Print:**	4 borders 2" x 38½", 4 borders 1½" x 24½", binding 1½" x 4½ yds.
⅞ yd.	**Green Solid:**	1 bias strip ¾" x 42", bias stripping ¾" x 8" for 4 B.
¼ yd.	**Green Print:**	68 F.
⅝ yd.	**Light Pink Print:**	8 M.
¼ yd.	**or Scraps in Various Green Prints:**	4 A, 4 C, 4 F, 16 K.
¼ yd.	**or Scraps in Various Flower Colors:**	4 D, 4 E, 4 Er, 20 G, 4 H, 16 I, 16 Ir, 16 J.
1 sk.	**Embroidery Floss:**	Green.
1⅛ yds.	**Lining.**	40" x 40" **Batting.**

1. Measure, mark, and cut a 20½" square (L) from white solid. Fold the square in half lengthwise and crosswise, and crease lightly. Place square over full-sized pattern on page 47, aligning dotted lines with folds. Mark the motif in each quarter of block, tracing whole I-J-Ir-K flower to finish incomplete flowers at edge of page.

2. Mark the border triangle pattern on this page in each of the 8 light pink M's.

3. Turn under ³⁄₁₆" and baste edges of appliqués. It is not necessary to turn under edges that will be covered by other patches. Turn under edges of bias strip for stems.

4. Position circular stem on block so that raw ends are located where a C leaf will cover them. Pin and blindstitch first outer edge, then inner edge. Position and appliqué patches on block in alphabetical order.

5. Position and appliqué patches on M triangles, also in alphabetical order.

6. Embroider stems and tendrils in outline stitch using 3 strands of embroidery floss.

7. Sew 4 short coral strips to block. Miter corners, trimming excess from seams.

8. Sew 3 striped M's alternately with 2 appliquéd M's. Sew to side of quilt. Repeat for other 3 sides. Add long coral borders. Miter corners, trimming excess from seams.

9. Quilt "in the ditch" around all appliqués and along border seam lines. Quilt along the stripes of the aqua M's. Use masking tape to mark 1" squares on the diagonal in the white background of the block. Quilt as marked. Bind in coral to finish.

BORDER TRIANGLE DIAGRAM

BORDER TRIANGLE PATTERN

Add ¼" seam allowances to M.

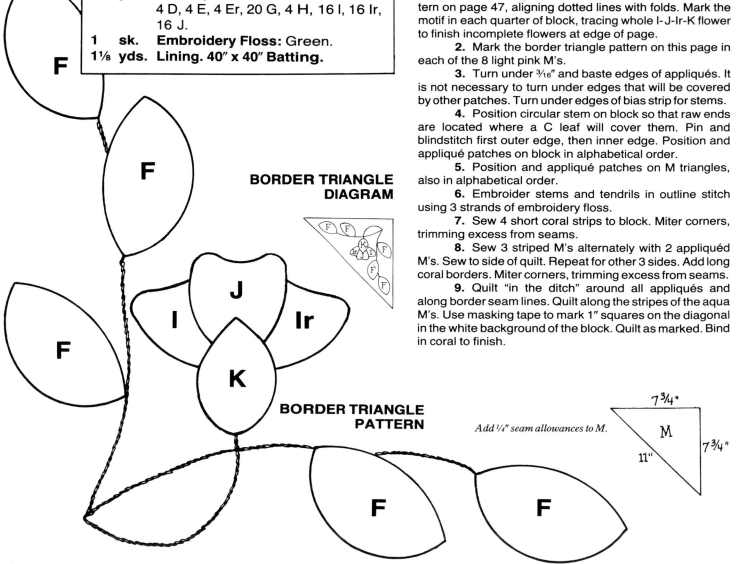

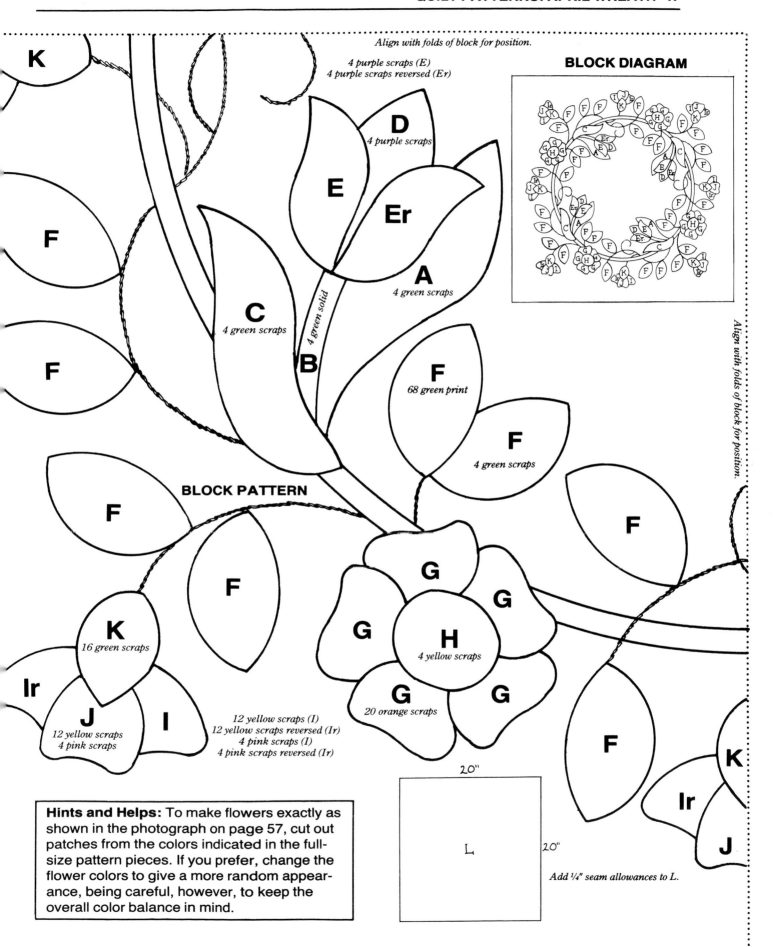

Align with folds of block for position.

4 purple scraps (E)
4 purple scraps reversed (Er)

BLOCK DIAGRAM

D
4 purple scraps

E

Er

A
4 green scraps

C
4 green scraps

B
4 green solid

F
68 green print

F
4 green scraps

BLOCK PATTERN

K
16 green scraps

F

F

F

F

F

Ir

J
12 yellow scraps
4 pink scraps

I

12 yellow scraps (I)
12 yellow scraps reversed (Ir)
4 pink scraps (I)
4 pink scraps reversed (Ir)

G

G

G

G

G

G

H
4 yellow scraps

20 orange scraps

F

K

Ir

J

20"

L

20"

Add ¼" seam allowances to L.

Align with folds of block for position.

Hints and Helps: To make flowers exactly as shown in the photograph on page 57, cut out patches from the colors indicated in the full-size pattern pieces. If you prefer, change the flower colors to give a more random appearance, being careful, however, to keep the overall color balance in mind.

TEXAS STAR

This appealing traditional pattern makes a good long-term project to pick up in odd moments. Each star can be cut out and hand sewn in fifteen minutes to a half hour. If you put together just one star per day in your spare time, you would have a very impressive quilt top completed in less than a year. The quilt is shown in color on page 33.

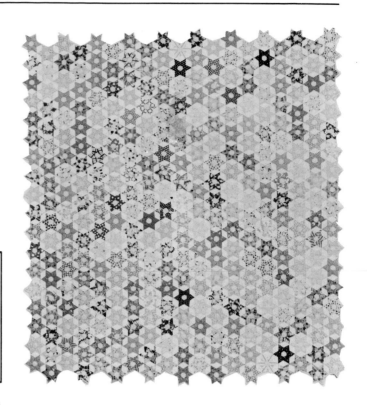

MATERIALS NEEDED

Quilt Size: 79¾" x 88".
2⅞ yds. White Solid: 953 C.
2 yds. Yellow Solid: binding 1½" x 15 yds., 342 B.
6¼ yds. or Scraps in Various Bright Prints: 2052 A.
5¼ yds. Lining. 84" x 92" Batting.

1. Referring to diagram, make 342 star units, each with 6 matching A's.
2. Join 18 stars point to point in a vertical row, with 17 diamonds (C's) inserted between stars. Repeat to make 19 vertical rows like this.
3. Join rows, staggering the stars so they touch point to point, inserting 35 diamonds between each two rows.
4. Outline quilt the patches ¼" in from seam lines of patches. Bind in yellow to finish.

Hints and Helps: Make all six points of a star from the same fabric. For a special touch, center a printed flower or other motif in each A patch of some of the stars when you cut out the patches. Stripes can also be used for special effects.

STAR UNIT

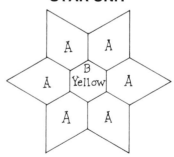

Arrows in pattern pieces indicate straight of grain.

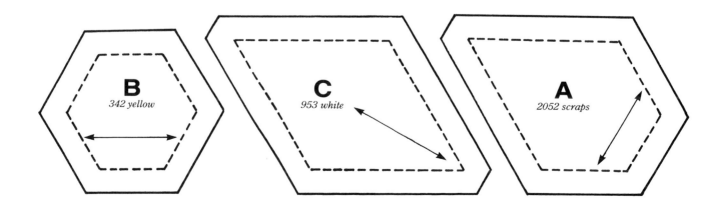

FANTASY VINE

Here is a new quilt with a '30s look, perfect for multicolored scraps in brights and pastels. It looks tricky, but it should be easily manageable for experienced quilters. See this quilt in color on page 39.

MATERIALS NEEDED

Quilt Size: 49¼" x 57½".
2½ yds. Cream Solid: 2 borders 3" x 60", 2 borders 3" x 51¾", 4 strips 2" x 52½", 30 C, 30 F, 30 H, 5 J, 5 K.
1⅝ yds. Blue Print: binding 1½" x 6½ yds., 2 borders 1½" x 55", 2 borders 1½" x 46¾", 8 strips 1½" x 52½".
1½ yds. or Scraps in Various Light Green Prints: 30 D, 30 E, 30 G, 30 I, 5 L.
¾ yd. or Scraps in Various Bright Prints: 30 A, 60 B.
3 yds. Lining. 53¼" x 61½" Batting.

1. Referring to diagrams, make 25 Unit 1's, 5 Unit 2's, and 5 Unit 3's.
2. Join 5 Unit 1's in a vertical row. Sew a Unit 2 to top and a Unit 3 to bottom to complete row. Make 5 rows.
3. Sew a 52½" blue strip to each edge of a 52½" cream strip. Repeat to make 4 of these sash units.
4. Sew block rows and sash units alternately.
5. Sew a short blue border strip to a short cream border strip, matching centers. Sew to top of quilt, with blue on inside edge, again matching centers. Repeat for bottom of quilt. Sew a long blue border to a long cream border, matching centers. Sew to side of quilt. Repeat for other side. Miter corners, trimming excess from seams.
6. Quilt "in the ditch" around patches in flower blocks and between strips. Quilt 1" squares on the diagonal in the cream background. Bind to finish.

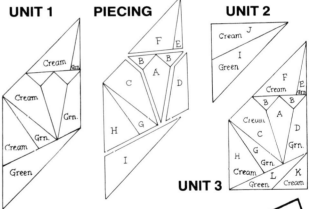

UNIT 1   PIECING   UNIT 2

UNIT 3

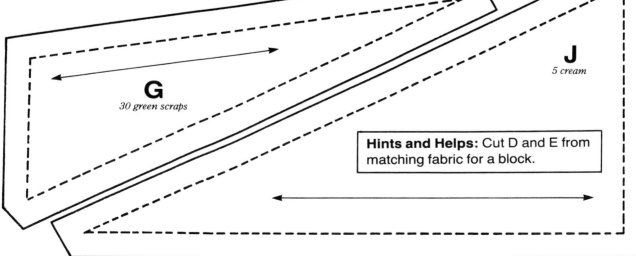

G
30 green scraps

J
5 cream

Hints and Helps: Cut D and E from matching fabric for a block.

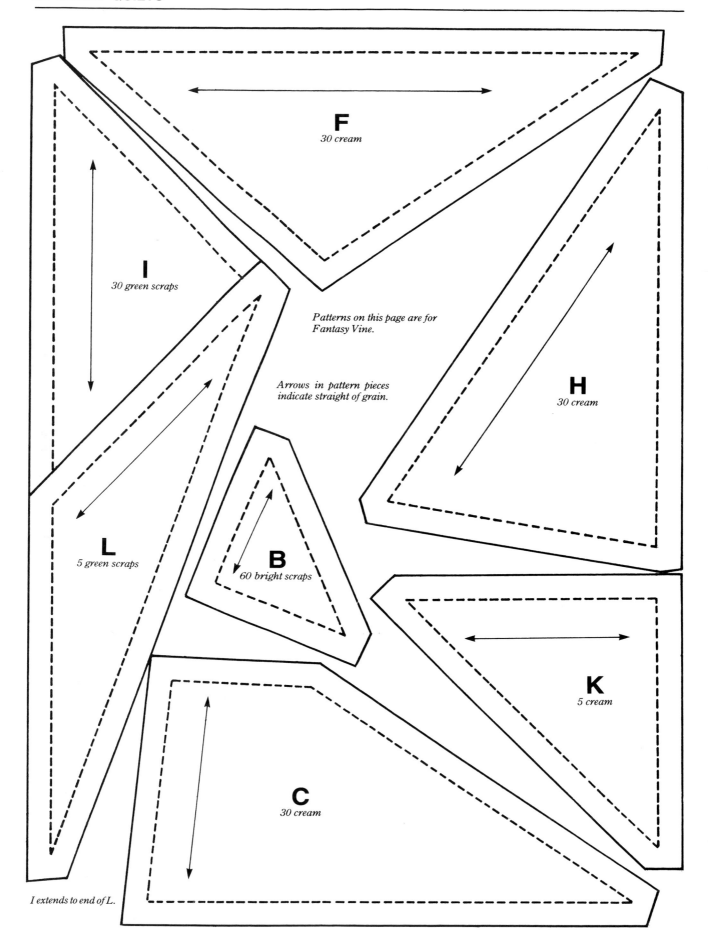

F
30 cream

I
30 green scraps

Patterns on this page are for *Fantasy Vine.*

Arrows in pattern pieces indicate straight of grain.

H
30 cream

L
5 green scraps

B
60 bright scraps

K
5 cream

C
30 cream

I extends to end of L.

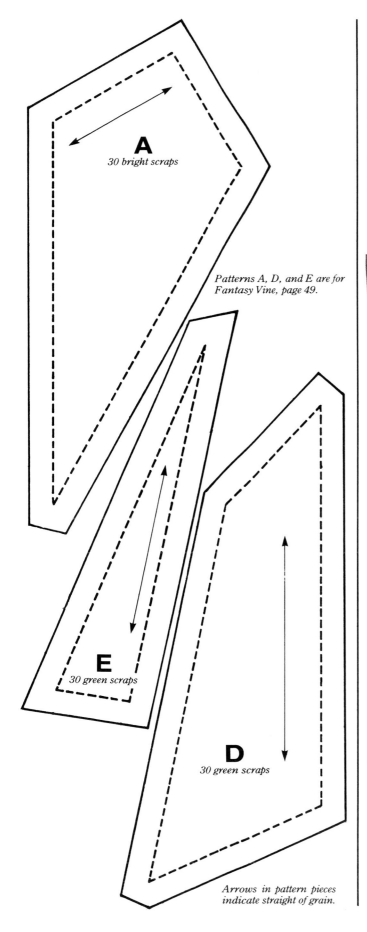

A

30 bright scraps

Patterns A, D, and E are for Fantasy Vine, page 49.

E

30 green scraps

D

30 green scraps

Arrows in pattern pieces indicate straight of grain.

JUDY'S FLOWER PATCH

Here's a quilt that can be cut out and pieced in just a few short hours. Make it as a companion wall hanging to the Judy's Flower Patch bed quilt (page 38) or make it as a gift to celebrate a special moment with someone you love. The wall quilt (page 39) is made from three blocks, but you could just as easily make a single flower or a half-dozen. Seven blocks side by side make a unique "pillow quilt," to go with the bed quilt.

MATERIALS NEEDED

Quilt Size: 32″ x 23″.

⅜ yd.	**Green Solid:** 3 H.	
½ yd.	**Muslin:** 6 B, 3 D, 3 Dr, 6 G, 6 I, 3 K, 3 Kr, 6 M, 3 N.	
1 yd.	**Dark Pink Print:** 2 borders 3″ x 34½″, 2 borders 3″ x 25½″.	
½ yd.	**Dark Pink Dot:** binding 1½″ x 3½ yds.	
⅜ yd.	**or Scraps in Various Dark Green Prints:** 6 G, 6 J, 3 L, 3 Lr.	
¼ yd.	**or Scraps in Various Dark Pink Prints:** 3 A, 3 C, 3 Cr, 3 E, 3 Er, 3 F.	
¼ yd.	**or Scraps in Various Green or Pink Prints:** 12 O.	
⅞ yd.	**Lining. 36″ x 27″ Batting.**	

1. Referring to diagram on page 52, make 3 Unit 1's, substituting muslin pieces for lilac ones in diagram. Add O's to make 3 Unit 3's.

2. Join the 3 Unit 3's in a row. Add borders, mitering corners and trimming excess from seams.

3. Quilt "in the ditch" around patches. Outline quilt ¼″ in from seam lines of O's and along border seams. Use masking tape to mark and quilt ¾″ squares on the diagonal in the muslin backgrounds of the blocks.

4. Bind in dark pink dot to finish.

JUDY'S FLOWER PATCH

This quilt looks impressive, but the piecing is really just basic straight seams, suitable for the sewing machine. The flowers could be made from multicolored scraps in brights and pastels for an equally charming look. Be sure to see the color picture on page 38 and the companion wall hanging on page 39.

MATERIALS NEEDED

Quilt Size: 90" x 94½".

4½ yds.	**Light Lilac Print:**	86 B, 43 D, 43 Dr, 86 G, 86 I, 43 K, 43 Kr, 86 M, 43 N.
2⅝ yds.	**Green Print:**	43 L, 43 Lr.
⅜ yd.	**Green Solid:**	43 H.
¾ yd.	**Lilac Solid:**	binding 1½" x 11½ yds.
2⅜ yds.	**or Scraps in Various Medium Blue/ Purple Prints:**	158 O.
2⅜ yds.	**or Scraps in Various Light Blue/ Purple Prints:**	158 O.
1 yd.	**or Scraps in Various Green Prints:**	86 G, 86 J.
1⅛ yds.	**or Scraps in Various Dark Pink/ Purple Prints:**	43 A, 43 C, 43 Cr.
1½ yds.	**or Scraps in Various Medium Dark Pink/Purple Prints:**	43 E, 43 Er, 43 F.
8 yds.	**Lining. 94" x 98½" Batting.**	

1. Referring to diagrams, make 43 Unit 1's.
2. Sew 4 O's to a Unit 1 to make Unit 2 as shown. Make 18 Unit 2's. Sew 4 O's to the corners of a Unit 1 to make Unit 3. Make 21 Unit 3's. Also make 2 Unit 4's, 2 Unit 5's, 4 Unit 6's, 10 Unit 7's, 6 Unit 8's, and 2 Unit 9's as shown.
3. Join Units 2, 6, and 7 in diagonal rows as shown in the quilt diagram to form rectangular center of quilt.

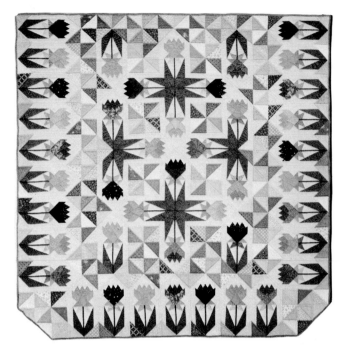

4. Join six Unit 8's end to end and sew to top of quilt center.
5. Being careful to keep all flowers right side up, Join 8 Unit 3's; add Unit 5; sew to side of quilt. Join 8 Unit 3's; add Unit 4; sew to opposite side. For bottom of quilt, join 5 Unit 3's; add Unit 4 to the left end and Unit 5 to the right end; attach.
6. Miter corners where Units 4 and 5 meet. Insert Unit 9's to fill in corners.
7. Quilt "in the ditch" around patches. Outline quilt ¼" from seam lines in O patches. Bind in lilac solid to finish.

UNIT 2   UNIT 3   UNIT 4   UNIT 5

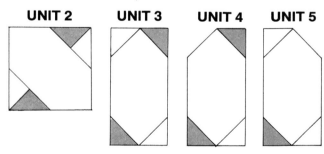

QUILT DIAGRAM   UNIT 1   PIECING   UNIT 7   UNIT 6   UNIT 8   UNIT 9

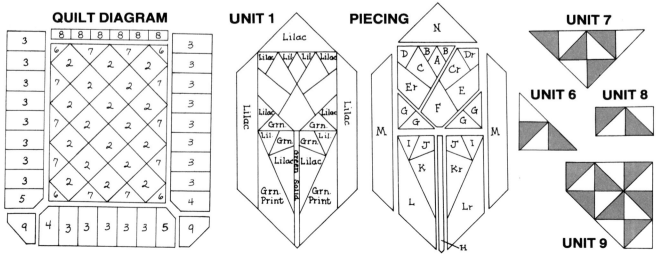

(Quantities in parentheses are for wall quilt.)

Arrows in pattern pieces indicate straight of grain.

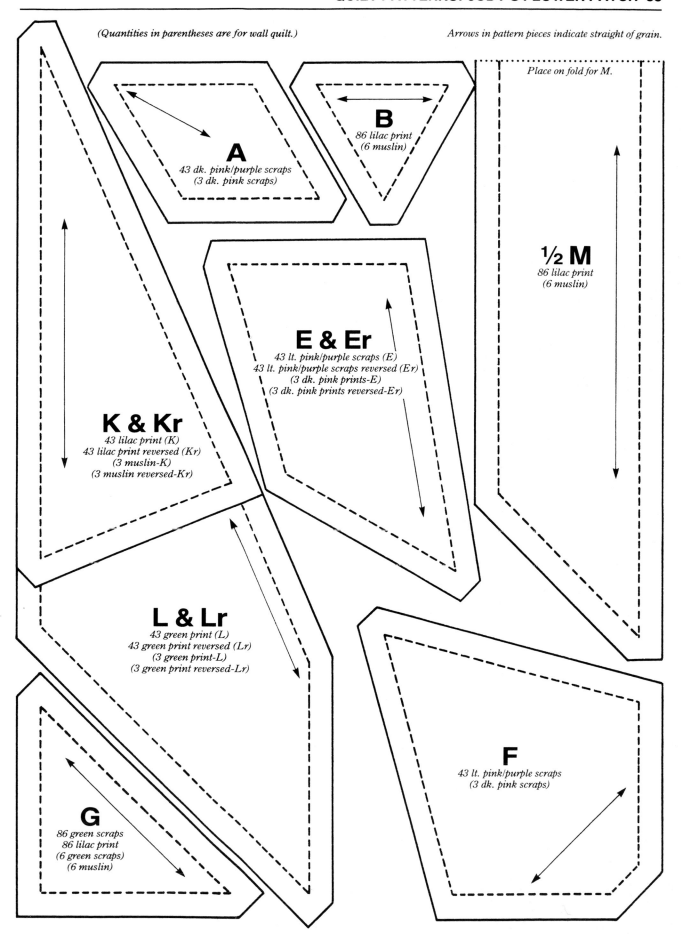

A

43 dk. pink/purple scraps
(3 dk. pink scraps)

B

86 lilac print
(6 muslin)

Place on fold for M.

½ M

86 lilac print
(6 muslin)

E & Er

43 lt. pink/purple scraps (E)
43 lt. pink/purple scraps reversed (Er)
(3 dk. pink prints-E)
(3 dk. pink prints reversed-Er)

K & Kr

43 lilac print (K)
43 lilac print reversed (Kr)
(3 muslin-K)
(3 muslin reversed-Kr)

L & Lr

43 green print (L)
43 green print reversed (Lr)
(3 green print-L)
(3 green print reversed-Lr)

G

86 green scraps
86 lilac print
(6 green scraps)
(6 muslin)

F

43 lt. pink/purple scraps
(3 dk. pink scraps)

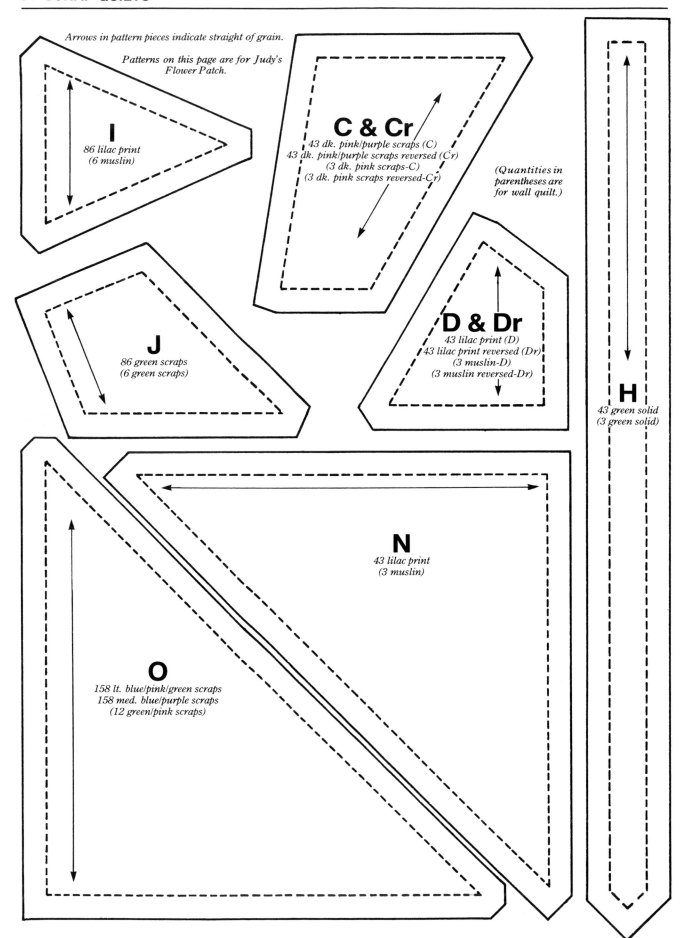

Arrows in pattern pieces indicate straight of grain.

Patterns on this page are for Judy's Flower Patch.

I

*86 lilac print
(6 muslin)*

C & Cr

*43 dk. pink/purple scraps (C)
43 dk. pink/purple scraps reversed (Cr)
(3 dk. pink scraps-C)
(3 dk. pink scraps reversed-Cr)*

(Quantities in parentheses are for wall quilt.)

J

*86 green scraps
(6 green scraps)*

D & Dr

*43 lilac print (D)
43 lilac print reversed (Dr)
(3 muslin-D)
(3 muslin reversed-Dr)*

H

*43 green solid
(3 green solid)*

N

*43 lilac print
(3 muslin)*

O

*158 lt. blue/pink/green scraps
158 med. blue/purple scraps
(12 green/pink scraps)*

STACKED BRICKS

A cross between Flying Geese and a herringbone pattern, this quilt is as easy to make as it is handsome. It would make a perfect charm quilt with 248 different dark prints on a muslin background. Yardage for two different sizes are given here. The smaller size is ideal for an afghan or wall hanging. The larger size makes a twin or double-bed coverlet. For a color picture of Stacked Bricks, see page 40.

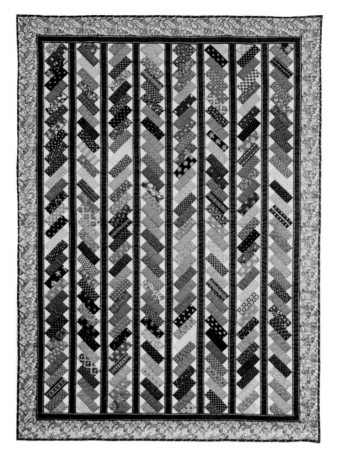

MATERIALS NEEDED

Quilt Size: 52½" x 72½".
2 yds. Brown Stripe: 2 borders 1⅞" x 69", 2 borders 1⅞" x 48⅞", 7 strips 1⅞" x 66¼", binding 1½" x 7½ yds.
2¼ yds. Brown Print: 2 borders 3½" x 75", 2 borders 3½" x 55".
2¼ yds. or Scraps in Various Dark Prints: 232 A, 8 B, 8 Br.
1⅜ yds. or Scraps in Various White/Light Prints: 464 C, 32 D.
3¼ yds. Lining. 56½" x 76½" Batting.

MATERIALS NEEDED

Quilt Size: 71¼" x 96⅞".
2⅝ yds. Brown Stripe: 2 borders 2½" x 91⅜", 2 borders 2½" x 64¾", 7 strips 2½" x 85⅜", binding 1½" x 10 yds.
2⅞ yds. Brown Print: 2 borders 4½" x 99⅜", 2 borders 4½" x 72¾".
3½ yds. or Scraps in Various Dark Prints: 232 A, 8 B, 8 Br.
2 yds. or Scraps in Various White/Light Prints: 464 C, 32 D.
5¾ yds. Lining. 75" x 101" Batting.

1. Referring to unit diagrams, make 108 Unit 1's, 8 Unit 2's, 108 Unit 3's, and 8 Unit 4's.

2. Join 27 Unit 1's to make a vertical row. Sew a Unit 2 to each end to complete Row 1. Repeat to make 4 rows like this.

3. Join 27 Unit 3's to make a vertical row. Sew a Unit 2 to each end to complete Row 2. Repeat to make 4 rows like this.

4. Sew a striped sash between Row 1 and Row 2. Repeat to make 4 strips like this. Join the strips with striped sashes between them.

5. Sew a short striped border to a short print border, matching centers. Sew to top of quilt. Repeat for bottom of quilt. Similarly sew a long striped border to a long print border and sew to side of quilt, matching centers. Re-

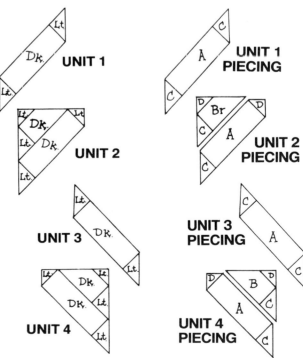

peat for other side. Miter corners, trimming excess from seam allowances.

6. Outline quilt or quilt "in the ditch" between patches and along border seams. Bind in brown stripe to finish.

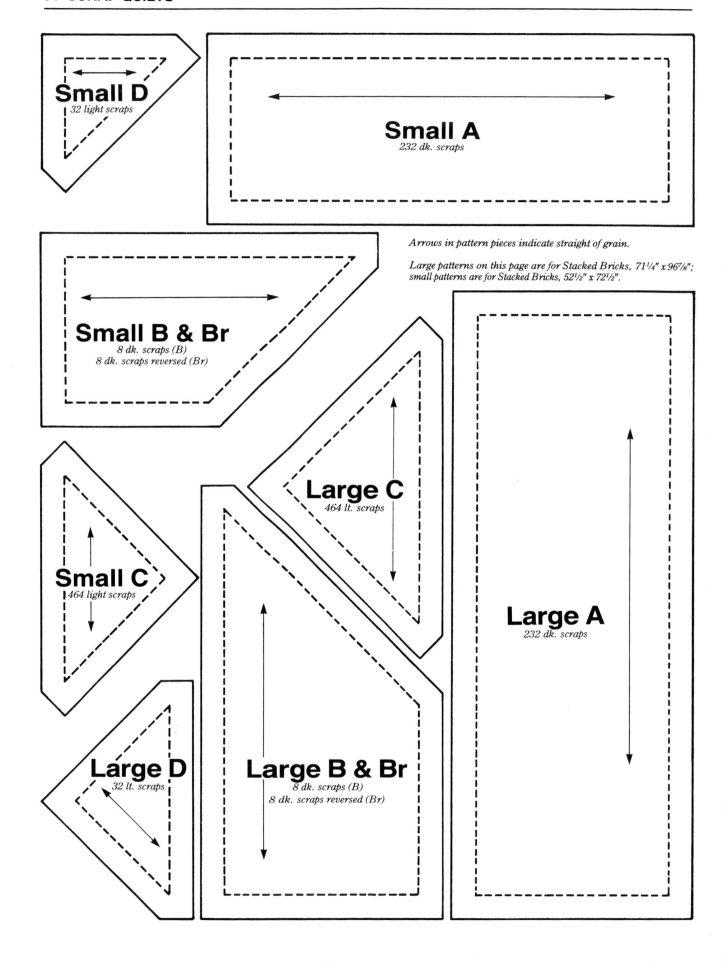

Small D
32 light scraps

Small A
232 dk. scraps

Arrows in pattern pieces indicate straight of grain.

Large patterns on this page are for Stacked Bricks, 71¼" x 96⅞"; small patterns are for Stacked Bricks, 52½" x 72½".

Small B & Br
8 dk. scraps (B)
8 dk. scraps reversed (Br)

Large C
464 lt. scraps

Large A
232 dk. scraps

Small C
464 light scraps

Large D
32 lt. scraps

Large B & Br
8 dk. scraps (B)
8 dk. scraps reversed (Br)

PLATE XXV: April Wreath, 35″ x 35″, original design by Susie Ennis and Judy Martin. Appliquéd and quilted by Jackie Madison; set together by Marie Shirer. Scraps of about 32 different pastel prints and 8-10 greens were used in the wreath. The appliquéd border triangles are identical to strengthen the framing effect of the border. An appealing striped fabric in the outer triangles unifies the color scheme and completes the medallion. Pattern is on page 46.

PLATE XXVI: Star ▶ of the Orient (Blue), 43″ x 43″, original design by Judy Martin. Pieced by Shirley Wegert; quilted by Margaret Waltz. This pattern is derived from an obscure Nancy Cabot design, "Unfolding Star." For this quilt, 81 blues were sorted into dark, medium, and light for careful arrangement in blocks and borders. The light background of blocks and borders was made from about 50 scrap prints ranging from white through beige. Gold scraps form block centers and setting squares. The brown sashes and borders unify the quilt. See Plate XXVII for a variation of this design. Pattern starts on page 68.

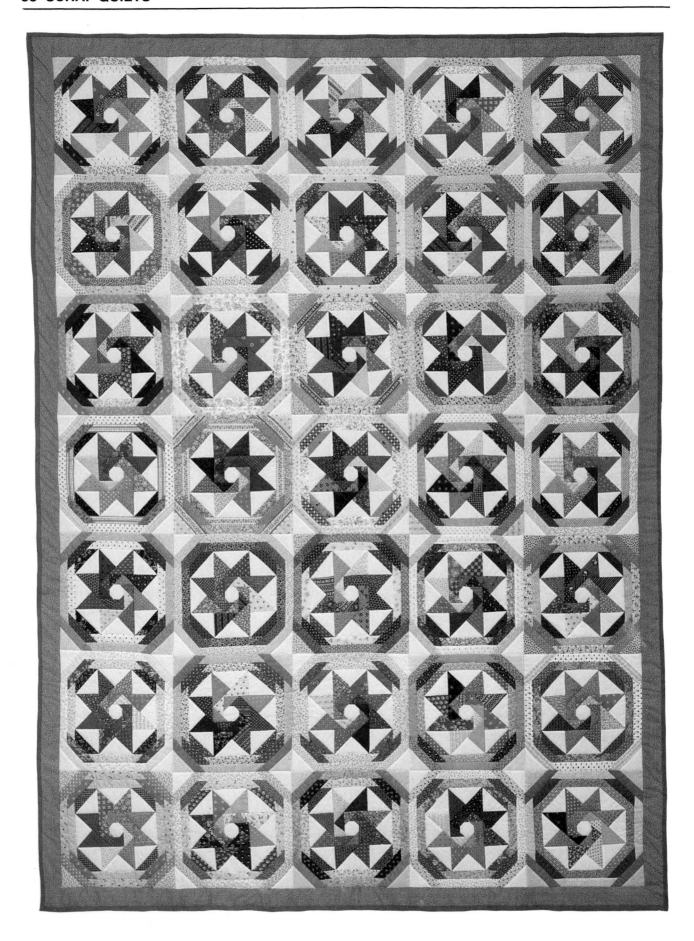

◄ **PLATE XXVIII:** Star Reel (Blue), 35″ x 35″, Judy Martin's original design combining a star with Virginia Reel blocks. Pieced by Judy Martin; quilted by Susan Harringa. Navy scraps of about 65 different prints, all reading about the same, were used. Compare this with Plate XXIX, below.

▼ **PLATE XXIX:** Star Reel (Brown), 35″ x 35″, the same original design as above. Pieced by Juanita Froese and Jeri Hoffmeyer; quilted by Judy Martin and Louise O. Townsend. About 135 prints ranging from brown through rust were used. To insure contrast with the various dark prints, a single light print was used throughout. Pattern is on page 71.

◄ **PLATE XXVII:** Star of the Orient (Rainbow), 75″ x 103″, original design by Judy Martin. Pieced by Reni Dieball; quilted by Gloria Oliver. A rainbow of colors in pastel tints, slightly grayed, was used. The muslin background offers relief. Each color must fit into the right slot in the rainbow, so the range within a color in the quilt is very small. About 200 different fabrics were used, 15-20 of each color. Pattern is on page 68.

PLATE XXX: Tennessee Waltz, 71″ x 89″, original arrangement combining two traditional blocks. Pieced by Louise O. Townsend; quilted by Susan Harringa. Scraps of 64 fabrics ranging from forest green through wine red, all clear and bright enough to contrast with the black star points and dark enough to show up against the tan print, were carefully selected. The small cream-colored squares provide the spark of light that lets the dark scraps sing. Pattern on page 74.

PLATE XXXI: Maltese Circles, 76″ x 96″, traditional Maltese Cross block in a new arrangement reminiscent of a Double Wedding Ring. Pieced and quilted by Carol Sears. Each of the 63 blocks is made using a different pastel print. Bright triangles in blocks and bright squares in pieced sashes are randomly placed to lead the eye through the quilt. About 160 prints were used. Colors (both pastel and bright) are clear primary and secondary colors. Pattern is on page 76.

PLATE XXXII: Colorado Log Cabin, 76″ x 100″, original design by Judy Martin. Pieced by Marla Stefanelli; quilted by Margaret Waltz. Blocks, each half light and half dark, are arranged in a Barn Raising set. Darks and lights include greens, browns, purples, and blacks or grays. About 100 dark prints and 100 light prints were used. Pattern is on page 78.

PLATE XXXIII: Yank's Irish Chain, 81″ x 97½″, a slight variation of a traditional Irish Chain. Pieced by Reni Dieball; quilted by Shirley Ann Holbrook. About 220 different pastel and light prints of all colors were used. Of the prints with white or natural background colors, only those with more figure than background were used. The solid red and blue are substantially darker and brighter than the prints so that the chains will stand out. Pattern is on page 80.

PLATE XXXIV: Country Cousin, 78″ x 94″. Judy Martin's original design resembles a traditional Fox and Geese block (page 90); however, the quilt setting and coloring more strongly resemble Birds in the Air (page 88). Pieced by Ann Elliott; quilted by Louise Morrison. Because this is basically a counterchange pattern in one color and white, it was possible to maintain the necessary contrast while varying the shades more than usual. About 70 different lights, ranging from white to dark beige, and 100 darks, ranging from red to rust, were used. The broad interpretation adds surface interest and gives the quilt an old-fashioned charm. Pattern is on page 82.

ARROWROOT MEDALLION

A border of serpentine vines adds the classic finishing touch to this quilt of pieced and appliquéd blocks. The quilt looks impressive, but the appliqué is very simple and the piecing is no harder than the average quilt. Choose your colors well, and this quilt will be a treasured heirloom. Since it is small, it is relatively quick to make. The quilt is shown in color on page 37.

MATERIALS NEEDED

Block Size: 15". Quilt Size: 63" x 63".

1⅞ yds.	**Red Print:** 4 borders 3½" x 65½".
¾ yds.	**Dark Green Print #1:** binding 1½" x 7¾ yds.
1⅜ yds.	**Dark Green Print #2:** 4 bias strips ¾" x 59".
1⅞ yds.	**Light Green Solid:** 4 borders 5" x 59½", 36 B, 36 C.
2¼ yds.	**or Scraps in Various Red Prints:** 45 A, 72 B, 48 D, 84 F.
1 yd.	**or Scraps in Various Green Prints:** 32 E, 188 F, 36 G.
⅝ yd.	**or Scraps in Various Gold Prints:** 36 A, 32 E.
3⅞ yds.	**Lining. 67" x 67" Batting.**

1. Cut 36 bias strips ¾" x 4½" from assorted green prints for G's. Turn under edges of appliqués and bias stripping for stems ³⁄₁₆" and baste.

2. Position C patches over full-size pattern to mark position for appliqués. Pin, baste, and appliqué G, then 3 F's on C. Repeat for each of 36 C's.

3. Referring to block diagram, make 9 blocks. Join blocks in 3 rows of 3 blocks.

4. Join E-D-EE-D-EE-D-E, making E's the right color to complete the 4-patches at top of quilt. Sew to top of quilt. Repeat for bottom of quilt. Join EE-D-EE-D-EE-D-EE and sew to one side of quilt. Repeat for other side.

5. Fold a border strip in half crosswise. Crease lightly to mark center line. Measure and crease to mark three segments of 7½"on each side of the center line.

6. Make a tracing of the 7½" border appliqué motif given on page 67. Mark the motif in half of the segments and the motif reversed (turned over, not rotated) in the other half, referring to quilt photo. The vines should end near the inner edge of border at corners. Mark all 4 border strips this way.

7. Sew borders to quilt, remembering that borders were cut with 2" extra length for insurance. Miter corners and trim excess from seams. Mark corner appliqué motifs.

8. Appliqué vines, then F's in the borders.

9. Add red print borders, mitering corners and trimming excess from seam allowances.

10. Outline quilt ¼" from seams of all pieced patches, but not crossing over tips of leaves in C's. Quilt

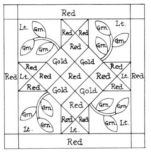

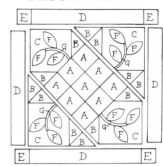

BLOCK   **BLOCK PIECING**

next to all appliqué patches. Use masking tape to mark and quilt 1" squares on the diagonal in the background of the light green borders and red borders, starting at the miter of each border. Bind in green to finish.

Hints and Helps: You may find it easier to keep the green and gold E squares in the proper positions for the 4-patches if you make the squares in the upper left and lower right corners of each block green (and make the squares in the other two corners gold). If you keep all the blocks turned the same direction, the 4-patches will fall into place perfectly.

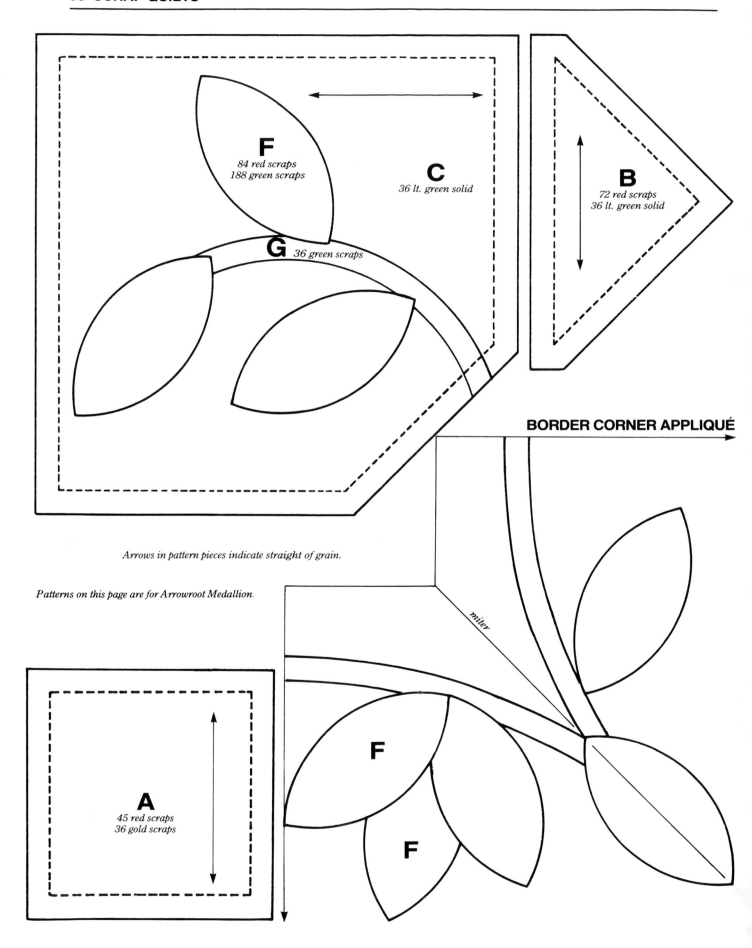

F
84 red scraps
188 green scraps

C
36 lt. green solid

G 36 green scraps

B
72 red scraps
36 lt. green solid

BORDER CORNER APPLIQUÉ

miter

Arrows in pattern pieces indicate straight of grain.

Patterns on this page are for Arrowroot Medallion.

A
45 red scraps
36 gold scraps

F

F

BORDER APPLIQUÉ

Arrows in pattern pieces indicate straight of grain.

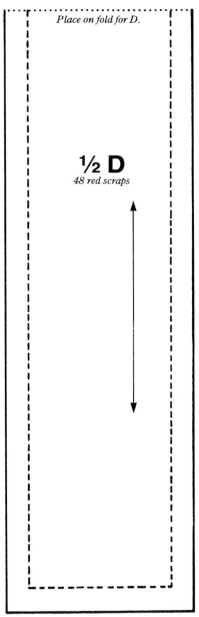

Place on fold for D.

½ D
48 red scraps

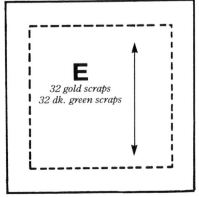

E
32 gold scraps
32 dk. green scraps

STAR OF THE ORIENT

This design has a 3-dimensional appearance reminiscent of origami, the oriental art of paper folding. The quilt looks complex, but the sewing is a breeze. Each star is made from eight colors, evenly spaced on the color wheel. Stars are turned so that different colors are on the top in each block, keeping the quilt lively. Star of the Orient is shown in color on page 58; a wall-hanging, also from this pattern, is on page 57.

MATERIALS NEEDED

Block Size: 14″. Quilt Size: 75″ x 103″.

2¼ yds.	**Muslin:**	35 A, 280 C, 68 I.
3 yds.	**Coral Print:**	2 borders 3″ x 105½″, 2 borders 3″ x 77½″.
¾ yd.	**Coral Solid:**	binding 1½″ x 10½ yds.
3 yds.	**or Scraps in Various Rainbow Pastels:**	280 B, 280 C.
1⅛ yds.	**or Scraps in Various Dark Yellow Prints:**	68 H, 72 I.
¾ yd.	**or Scraps in Various Dark Orange Prints:**	72 H.
⅝ yd.	**or Scraps in Various Dark Pink Prints:**	72 F.
½ yd.	**or Scraps in Various Dark Purple Prints:**	72 D.
½ yd.	**or Scraps in Various Dark Blue Prints:**	68 D.
⅝ yd.	**or Scraps in Various Dark Green Prints:**	68 F.
1 yd.	**or Scraps in Various Light Yellow Prints:**	68 G.
1 yd.	**or Scraps in Various Light Orange Prints:**	72 G.
⅞ yd.	**or Scraps in Various Light Pink Prints:**	72 E.
⅞ yd.	**or Scraps in Various Light Green Prints:**	68 E.
6⅛ yds.	**Lining.**	79″ x 107″ Batting.

1. Referring to block diagrams, Hint at right, and Piecing Sequence Figures on page 69, make 35 octagonal star units. Each star unit has 8 B's and 8 matching C's. (These are numbered 1-8 in the block diagrams to indicate placement of matching pairs.) Choose the 8 colors to range from pink through purple, blue, green, yellow, and orange, with in-between shades as well. Add D's, E's, F's, G's, H's, then I's in colors shown to complete 17 Y blocks and 18 Z blocks.

2. Join 3 Z blocks alternately with 2 Y blocks to make a row. Make 4 rows like this. Join 3 Y blocks alternately with 2 Z blocks to make a row. Make 3 rows like this.

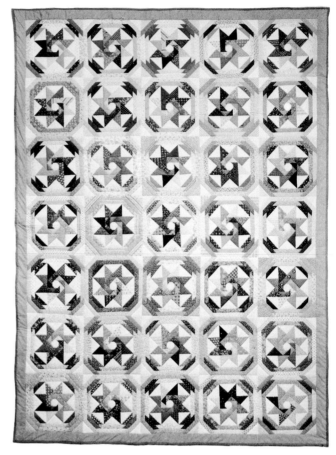

Join rows, alternating types.

3. Add borders, mitering corners and trimming excess from seam allowances.

4. Quilt "in the ditch" between patches, or outline quilt ¼″ from seam lines. Bind to finish.

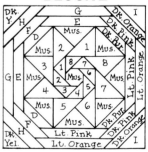

BLOCK Y **BLOCK Z**

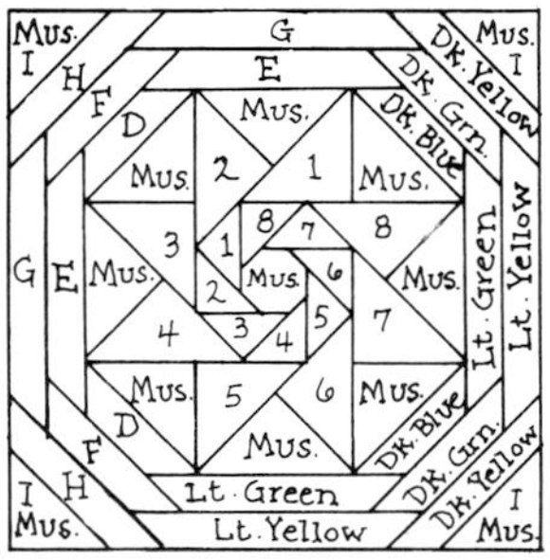

Hints and Helps: To make Unit 1, sew the first B to A only halfway down the side of the octagon. See the figures on page 69. Add 7 more B's (counterclockwise), then complete the first seam when joining the eighth B to the first B and A. Join Unit 2's to Unit 1's in a similar fashion.

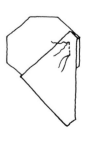

PIECING SEQUENCE FIGURES

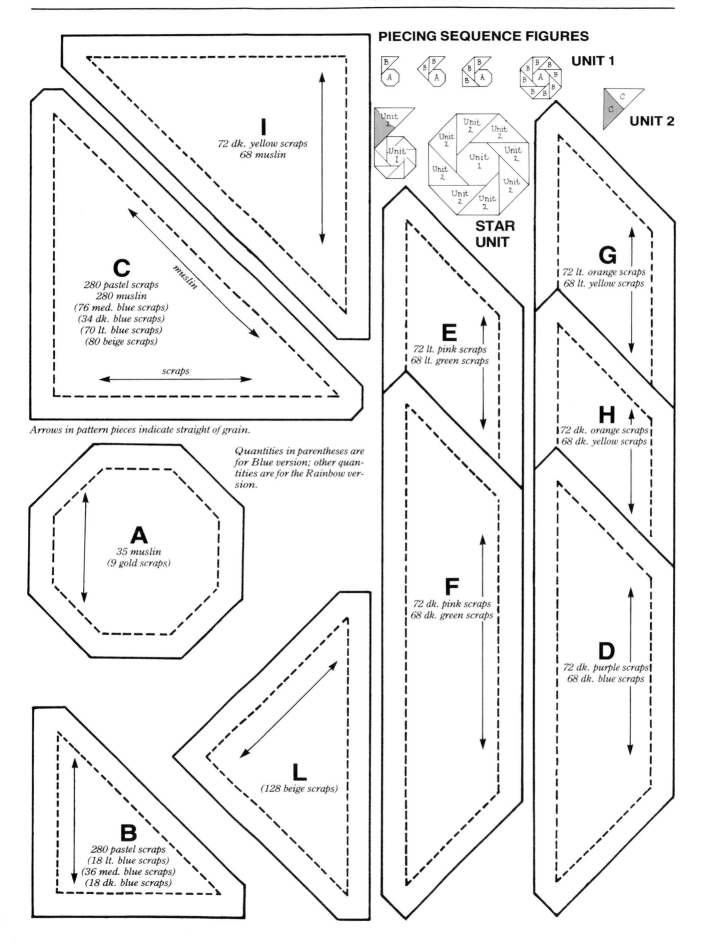

I

72 dk. yellow scraps
68 muslin

C

280 pastel scraps
280 muslin
(76 med. blue scraps)
(34 dk. blue scraps)
(70 lt. blue scraps)
(80 beige scraps)

muslin

scraps

Arrows in pattern pieces indicate straight of grain.

A

35 muslin
(9 gold scraps)

*Quantities in parentheses are
for Blue version; other quantities are for the Rainbow version.*

B

280 pastel scraps
(18 lt. blue scraps)
(36 med. blue scraps)
(18 dk. blue scraps)

L

(128 beige scraps)

UNIT 1

UNIT 2

STAR UNIT

G

72 lt. orange scraps
68 lt. yellow scraps

E

72 lt. pink scraps
68 lt. green scraps

H

72 dk. orange scraps
68 dk. yellow scraps

F

72 dk. pink scraps
68 dk. green scraps

D

72 dk. purple scraps
68 dk. blue scraps

STAR OF THE ORIENT

As different as it looks, this is just another version of the pattern on page 68. Thanks to its small size, this quilt is quick and easy to make. The Wild Goose Chase border is perfect for machine piecing. See this quilt in color on page 57.

MATERIALS NEEDED

Block Size: 10″. Quilt Size: 48¼″ x 48 ¼″.	
1½ yds.	**Brown Print:** 4 borders 3″ x 50¾″, 4 borders 1¾″ x 37½″, 12 J.
⅜ yd.	**or Scraps in Various Dark Blue Prints:** 18 B, 34 C.
¾ yd.	**or Scraps in Various Medium Blue Prints:** 36 B, 76 C.
¾ yd.	**or Scraps in Various Light Blue Prints:** 18 B, 70 C.
⅛ yd.	**or Scraps in Various Gold Prints:** 9 A, 4 K.
1¼ yds.	**or Scraps in Various Beige Prints:** 80 C, 128 L.
3 yds.	**Lining.** 52¼″ x 52¼″ **Batting.**

1. Referring to block diagram, Hint on page 68, and Piecing Sequence Figures on page 69, make an octagonal star unit and add light blue C's to the four corners to complete block. Make 9 blocks.

2. Join 3 blocks alternately with 2 J's to make a block row. Make 3 block rows.

3. Join 3 J's alternately with 2 K's to make a sash row. Make 2 sash rows. Join block rows and sash rows, alternating types.

4. Add narrow brown borders, mitering corners and trimming excess from seam allowances.

5. Referring to diagrams, make 4 Unit 3's and 4 Unit 4's.

6. Sew a Unit 3 to left side of quilt, with triangles pointing down. Sew another Unit 3 to right side of quilt, with triangles pointing up.

7. Sew a Unit 4 to each end of the two remaining Unit 3's. Sew to top and bottom of quilt, with triangles pointing left on top and right on the bottom border.

8. Add wide brown borders, mitering corners and trimming excess from seams.

9. Quilt "in the ditch" between patches or outline quilt, as desired. Bind to finish.

BLOCK

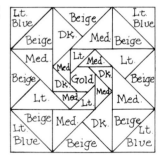

UNIT 3

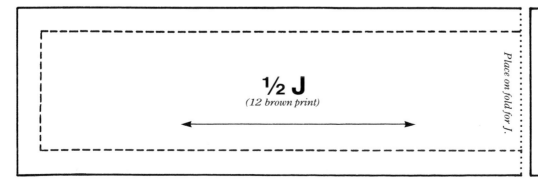

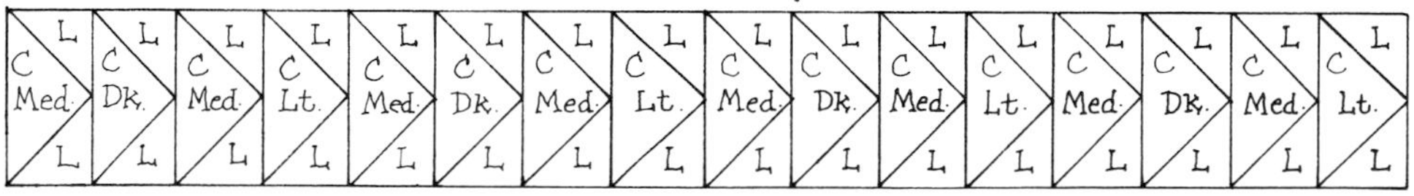

UNIT 4

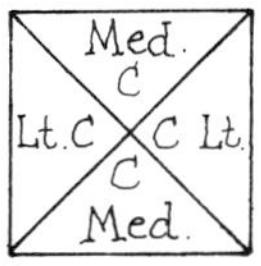

½ J
(12 brown print)

Place on fold for J.

K
(4 gold scraps)

STAR REEL

This fascinating quilt with its maze of scrolling "arms" looks tricky, but the sewing and the arrangement are really perfectly simple. A mere 35½" square, this quilt can be cut and sewn in a single day by an experienced piecer using chain-piecing techniques. (In fact, this one was cut and pieced in just five hours.) Two different versions of the quilt are shown in color on page 59.

MATERIALS NEEDED

Quilt Size: 35½" x 35½".
1¼ yds. Light Print or Solid: 8 C, 20 E, 16 F, 16 G, 16 H, 8 I, 16 J, 96 K.
⅝ yd. Dark Print: 8 N.
⅜ yd. Medium Dark Print: 8 M.
½ yd. Dark Print or Solid: binding 1½" x 4½ yds.
1 yd. or Scraps in Various Dark Prints: 1 A, 4 B, 16 D, 16 E, 16 F, 16 G, 16 H, 48 L.
1¼ yds. Lining. 39½" x 39½" Batting.

1. Referring to diagrams, make 1 Unit 1, 4 Unit 2's, 8 Unit 3's, 4 Unit 4's, 8 Unit 5's, and 40 Unit 6's.
2. Join 5 Unit 6's and a Unit 5 to make a strip. Add M, N, and J to complete Unit 7. Make 8 Unit 7's.
3. Join Units, D's, and I's as shown in the quilt diagram.
4. Quilt ¼" from seam line around the spiraling shapes in the light color. Echo quilt in concentric lines ¼" apart inside this area. Outline quilt ¼" from seams in the light K triangles in the borders. Quilt "in the ditch" along seam lines of M and N patches. Bind to finish.

Hints and Helps: To mark concentric lines for echo quilting, use ¼"-wide masking tape. Lay tape along all of the seam lines surrounding the area to be echo quilted. Quilt along the edge of the tape (¼" from seam lines), and move the tape to the other side of the line of quilting just completed to mark the quilting for the next row.

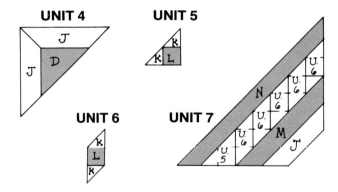

UNIT 4 **UNIT 5**

UNIT 6 **UNIT 7**

QUILT DIAGRAM

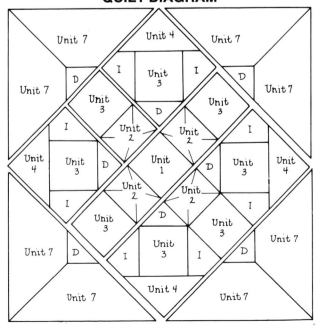

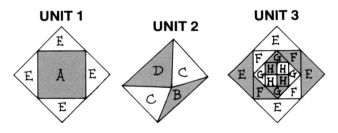

UNIT 1 **UNIT 2** **UNIT 3**

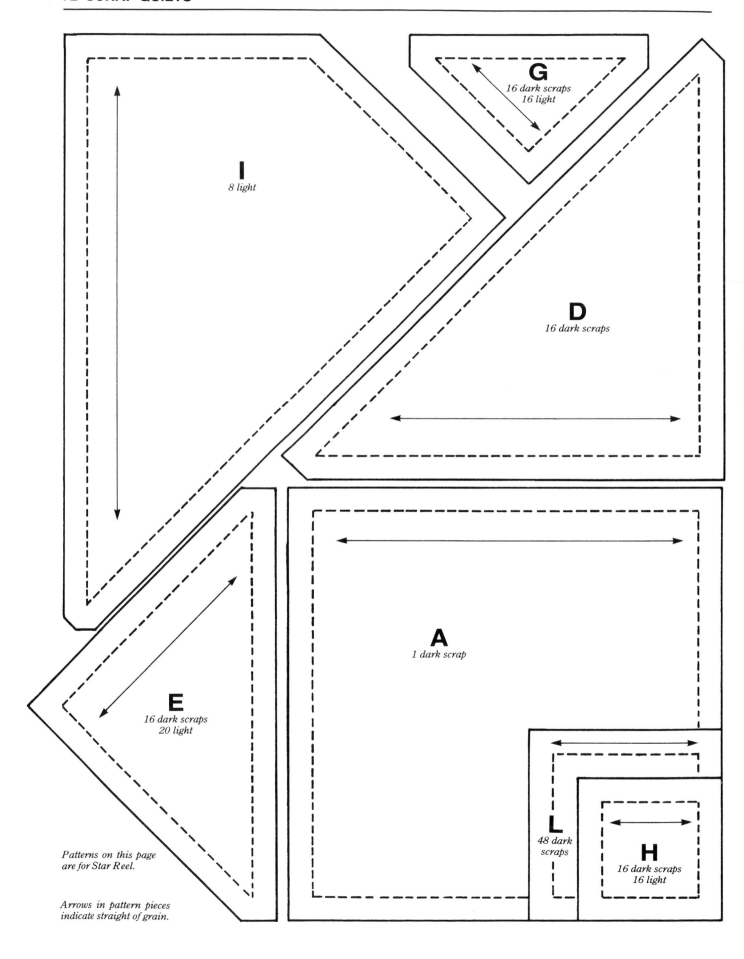

I
8 light

G
16 dark scraps
16 light

D
16 dark scraps

E
16 dark scraps
20 light

A
1 dark scrap

L
48 dark scraps

H
16 dark scraps
16 light

Patterns on this page are for Star Reel.

Arrows in pattern pieces indicate straight of grain.

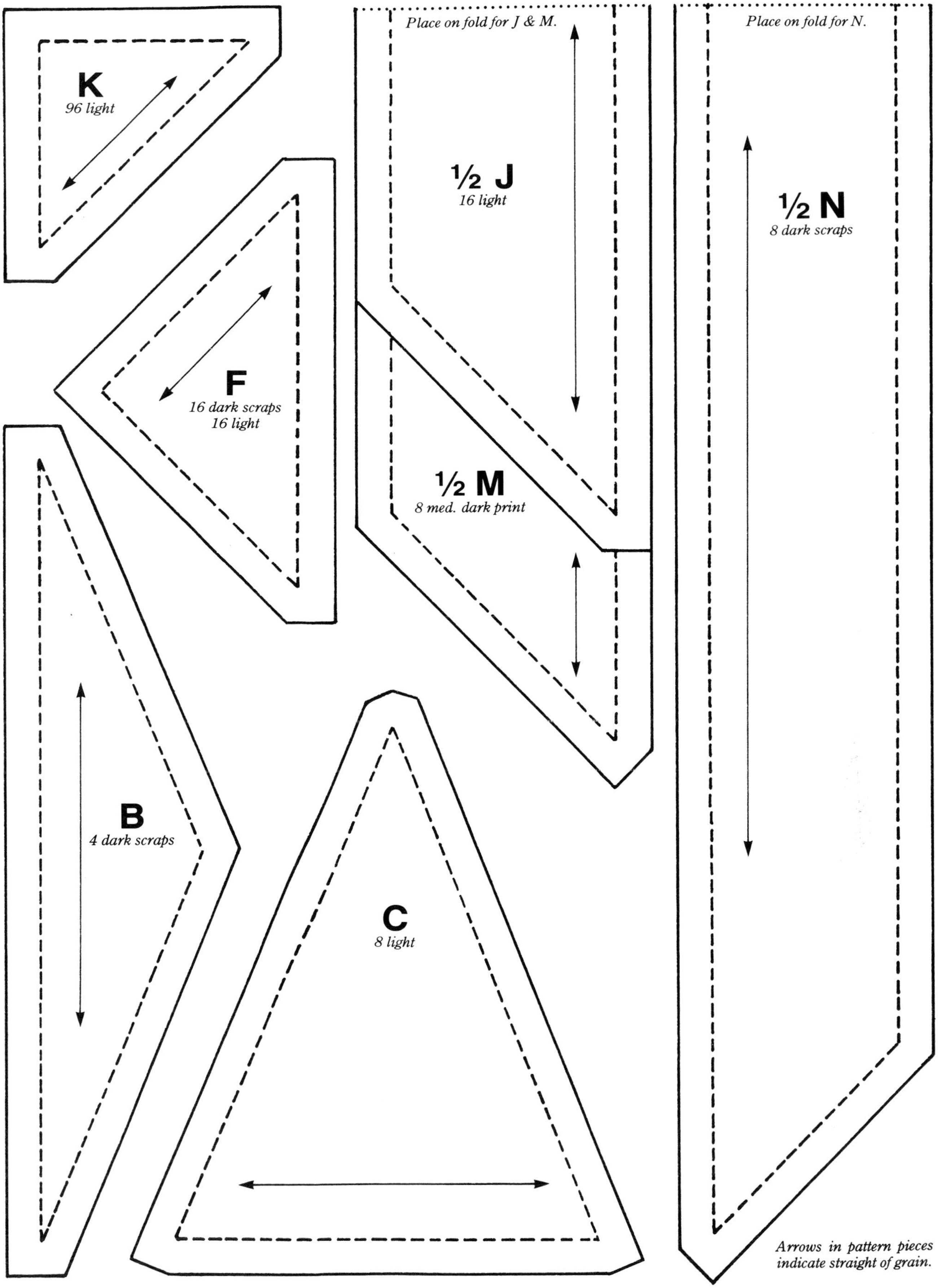

K
96 light

F
16 dark scraps
16 light

B
4 dark scraps

C
8 light

Place on fold for J & M.

½ J
16 light

½ M
8 med. dark print

Place on fold for N.

½ N
8 dark scraps

*Arrows in pattern pieces
indicate straight of grain.*

TENNESSEE WALTZ

Two traditional blocks, Snowball and 54-40 or Fight, are combined in this striking, easy-to-make quilt, which is shown in color on page 60. This is a good scrap quilt for one who has only a small fabric collection, since scraps make up only about one-sixth of the materials required for the quilt top.

MATERIALS NEEDED

Block Size: 9". Quilt Size: 71" x 89".

2¾ yds. **Black Print:** 2 borders 3" x 91½", 2 borders 3" x 73½", binding 1½" x 9½ yds., 128 E, 128 Er.

2½ yds. **Brown Stripe:** 2 borders 2" x 86½", 2 borders 2" x 68½"

3 yds. **Cream Solid:** 31 A, 256 D.

1⅝ yds. **Tan Print:** 124 B, 128 C.

1½ yds. **or Scraps in Various Dark Prints:** 384 D.

5⅜ yds. **Lining. 75" x 93" Batting.**

1. Referring to block drawings and piecing diagrams, make 31 Y blocks and 32 Z blocks.

2. Join four Z blocks alternately with three Y blocks to make a row. Make five rows like this. Join four Y blocks alternately with three Z blocks to make a row. Make four rows like this. Join rows, alternating types.

3. Sew a short striped border strip to a short black print border strip, matching centers. Sew to top of quilt with black print outside, again matching centers. Repeat for bottom of quilt. Similarly sew a long striped border to a long black print border and sew to side of quilt. Repeat for other side. Miter corners, trimming excess from seam allowances.

4. To make tracing pattern for quilting Y blocks, fold a 9" square of tracing paper in half. With black felt pen, trace half of the A pattern (with quilting) on one side of fold line, then complete pattern by tracing on other side of fold line. Position the tracing under A patch in quilt, and use pencil or water-erasable marker to mark quilting design lightly. Repeat for each A patch.

5. To make tracing pattern for quilting borders, trace a portion of the quilting motif given in the A patch as shown in Fig. 1. Measure and mark a dot ¼" below the lower point of each flower. Connect dots to make a line to represent outer seam line of quilt. Make another, parallel line 3" above this line to represent the inner seam line of the border. Fold the tracing in half so one flower aligns over the other. Crease to mark center line. Position the tracing with top and bottom aligned with inner and outer seam lines of border and center fold even with center of Y or Z block in quilt. Mark lightly onto border. Repeat opposite each block around the quilt's perimeter. Connect the motifs by tracing another scallop (from the same motif) from flower to flower along outer edge of border. Mark a single flower with four leaves over each miter at corners as

BLOCK Y

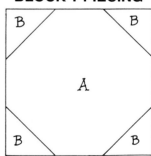

BLOCK Y PIECING

BLOCK Z

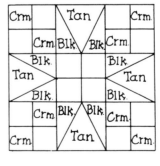

BLOCK Z PIECING

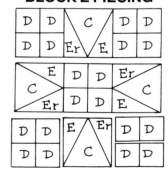

in Fig. 2. Connect these to neighboring motifs with extended scallop along inner edge.

6. Baste together top, lining, and batting. Quilt as marked. Outline quilt the patches. Bind to finish.

Arrows in pattern pieces indicate straight of grain.

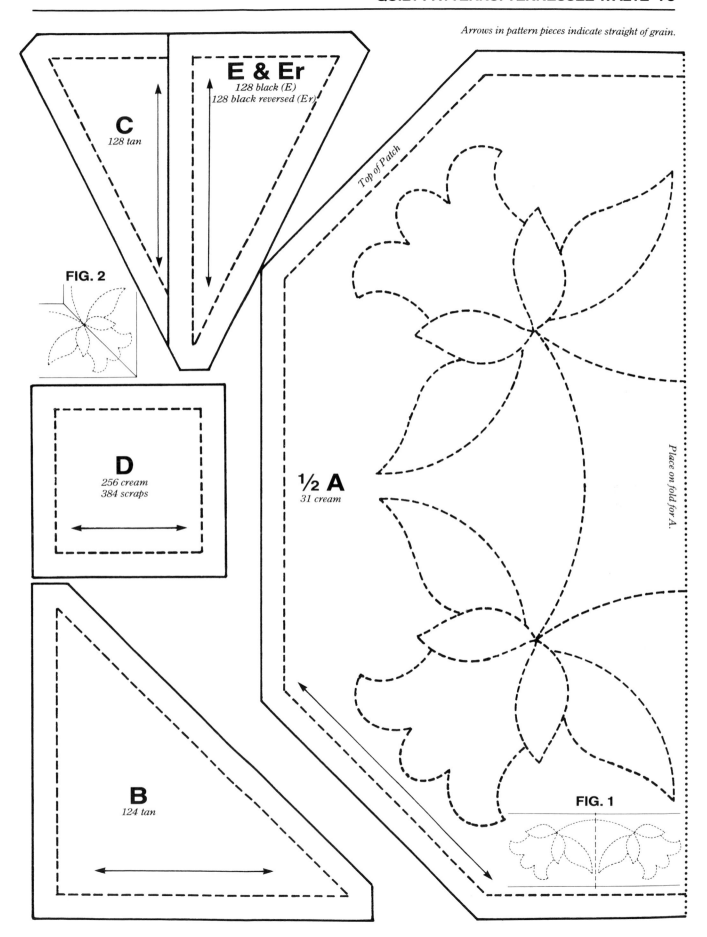

C
128 tan

E & Er
128 black (E)
128 black reversed (Er)

Top of Patch

FIG. 2

D
256 cream
384 scraps

½ A
31 cream

Place on fold for A.

B
124 tan

FIG. 1

MALTESE CIRCLES

Like a Double Wedding Ring, this quilt gives the impression of interlocked circles, but it is sewn in simple straight seams instead of tricky curves. A rainbow of colors is sorted carefully into brights and pastels arranged to strengthen the overall design. The quilt is shown in color on page 61.

MATERIALS NEEDED

Block Size: 7½". Quilt Size: 76" x 96".

¾ yd.	**Dark Yellow Print:** binding 1½" x 10¼ yds.
2⅞ yds.	**Blue Print:** 2 borders 3" x 98½", 2 borders 3" x 78½".
2¾ yds.	**Yellow Solid:** 2 borders 2¼" x 93½", 2 borders 2¼" x 73½", 63 A, 48 E.
1½ yds.	**Med. Yellow Print:** 220 E.
1¼ yds.	**Muslin:** 252 D.
2¾ yds.	**or Scraps in Various Pastel Prints:** 252 B.
2¼ yds.	**or Scraps in Various Bright Prints:** 252 C, 110 E.
5¾ yds.	**Lining. 80" x 100" Batting.**

1. Referring to block drawing and piecing diagram, make 63 blocks. Also make 110 sashes, as shown.
2. Join seven blocks alternately with six sashes to make a block row. Repeat to make nine block rows. Join seven sashes alternately with six yellow solid E's to make a sash row. Repeat to make eight sash rows. Join block rows and sash rows, alternating types.
3. Sew a short yellow border strip to a short blue border strip, matching centers. Sew to top of quilt, again matching centers. Repeat for bottom of quilt. Similarly sew a long yellow border to a long blue border and sew to side of quilt, matching centers. Repeat for other side. Miter corners, trimming excess from seam allowances.
4. Outline quilt or quilt "in the ditch" around patches and along border seam lines. Bind in dark yellow print to finish.

SASH

Yellow Print	Bright	Yellow Print

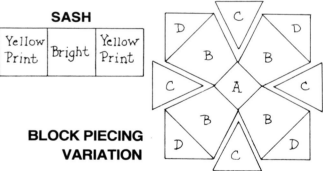

BLOCK PIECING VARIATION

Hints and Helps: Make all four B's in a block from the same fabric, but place C's randomly. This will enhance both the Maltese Cross pattern and the interlocked circles pattern in the quilt. Make all the blocks and sashes before setting any of them together. Lay out blocks and sashes on the floor to distribute colors evenly.

There are a couple of ways to piece this block. You may want to experiment with these to see which method you prefer: (1) Sew B's to two opposite sides of A. Add D's. Sew C's to two opposite sides of each remaining B. Add D's. Join segments. (2) Sew 4 B's to A, sewing only to end of seam line, not to edges of patches. Insert 4 C's, stitching from wide end to point. Add four D's.

BLOCK

BLOCK PIECING

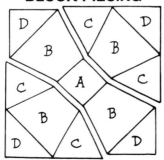

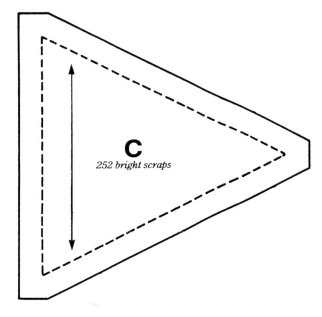

C

252 bright scraps

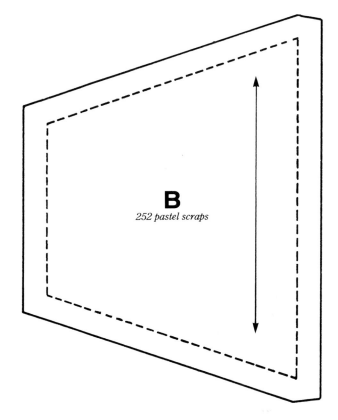

B

252 pastel scraps

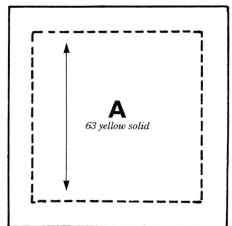

A

63 yellow solid

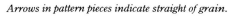

Arrows in pattern pieces indicate straight of grain.

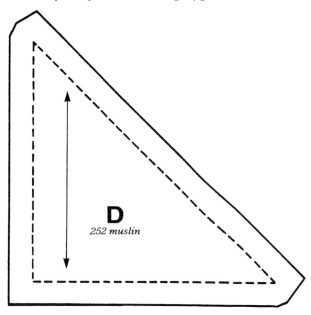

D

252 muslin

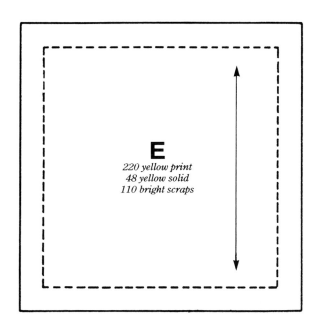

E

220 yellow print
48 yellow solid
110 bright scraps

COLORADO LOG CABIN

Here is a Log Cabin with a difference: stars are formed where the blocks meet. No matter what Log Cabin setting arrangement you choose, the stars appear creating a lovely secondary pattern. The sewing is no harder than a Lemoyne Star, easy enough for a careful beginner. With all of its fascinating possibilities, Colorado Log Cabin ought to keep the more experienced quiltmaker interested as well. See a color picture on page 62.

MATERIALS NEEDED

Block Size: 12". Quilt Size: 76" x 100".

1	yd.	**Dark Gold Print:** 48 A, 192 H.
⅞	yd.	**Medium Gold Print:** 192 H.
3	yds.	**Purple Stripe:** 2 borders 2½" x 102½", 2 borders 2½" x 78½".
½	yd.	**Brown Print:** binding 1½" x 10½ yds.
4	yds.	**or Scraps in Various Dark Prints:** 48 B, 48 C, 48 D, 48 E, 48 F, 48 G, 96 I.
3½	yds.	**or Scraps in Various Light Prints:** 48 A, 48 B, 48 C, 48 D, 48 E, 48 F, 96 I.
5⅞	yds.	**Lining. 80" x 104" Batting.**

1. Referring to block drawing and piecing diagram, sew patches in alphabetical order from A-G, spiraling clockwise from the center. Sew a dark gold H to one end of each I, and a medium gold H to the opposite end, being careful always to place the dark gold H on the same end. Make three more H-I-H pieces, and attach one to each side of block center, mitering corners to complete block. Make 48 blocks.
2. Arrange blocks in four rows of six blocks each. Turn blocks so that light/dark pattern matches the color photo of the quilt, or experiment with another arrangement of your own.
3. Being careful to keep blocks turned according to your plan, join six blocks into a row. Repeat to make eight rows. Join rows.
4. Add borders, mitering corners and trimming excess from seam allowances.
5. Quilt "in the ditch" between patches or outline quilt ¼" from seam lines. Quilt along border seam lines. Bind in brown to finish.

BLOCK   **BLOCK PIECING**

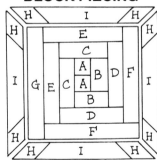

Hints and Helps: Sort your scraps into lights and darks, but be sure to include a few nearly medium shades for variety. It is more interesting to use more than one color (this quilt has brown, green, and purple) in both the lights and the darks.

Like any other Log Cabin design, this quilt has many setting options. The arrangement shown is called a Barn Raising. Diagonal bands of light and dark (called Straight Furrows) or alternating crosses of light and dark (Sunshine and Shadows) are just two of the other arrangements possible.

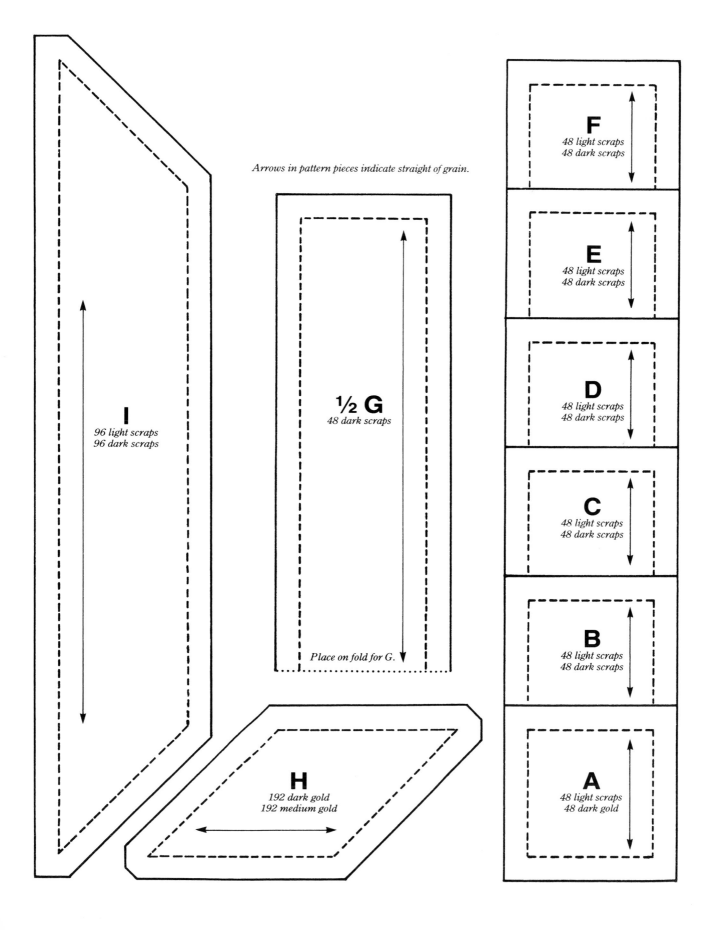

Arrows in pattern pieces indicate straight of grain.

I
96 light scraps
96 dark scraps

½ G
48 dark scraps

Place on fold for G.

H
192 dark gold
192 medium gold

F
48 light scraps
48 dark scraps

E
48 light scraps
48 dark scraps

D
48 light scraps
48 dark scraps

C
48 light scraps
48 dark scraps

B
48 light scraps
48 dark scraps

A
48 light scraps
48 dark gold

YANK'S IRISH CHAIN

This delightful design is one of the easiest ever to piece. Choosing colors for it is a joy, too, with all of your splashy multicolored prints fitting in perfectly. A striking pieced border and a luscious new quilting pattern for the muslin spaces make Yank's Irish Chain a stand-out. The quilt is shown in a room setting, in color, on page 63.

MATERIALS NEEDED

Block Size: 12¼". Quilt Size: 81¼" x 97½".
2¼ yds. Muslin: 17 A, 68 B, 72 C.
2½ yds. Red Solid: binding 1½" x 10½ yds., 493 C.
2⅞ yds. Blue Solid: 2 strips 3½" x 98¼", 2 strips 2¼" x 90", 2 strips 3½" x 83¾", 1 strip 2¼" x 83¾", 1 strip 2¼" x 67¼", 72 C.
3⅝ yds. or Scraps in Various Pastel Prints: 878 C.
5⅞ yds. Lining. 85" x 102" Batting.

1. Referring to block and unit drawings and piecing diagrams, make 17 Y blocks, 18 Z blocks, 70 Unit 1's, 71 Unit 2's, and 2 Unit 3's.
2. Join 3 Z blocks alternately with 2 Y blocks to make a row. Make four rows like this. Join 3 Y blocks alternately with 2 Z blocks to make a row. Make three rows like this. Join rows, alternating types.
3. Sew shortest narrow border to bottom of quilt. Sew longest narrow borders to sides of quilt. Miter two lower corners, trimming excess from seams.
4. Sew 25 Unit 1's alternately with 25 Unit 2's, being careful to turn Unit 2's so red squares zigzag down the length of the border. Sew to side of quilt. Repeat for other side. Sew 21 Unit 2's alternately with 20 Unit 1's, again being careful how you turn the Unit 2's. Sew a Unit 3 to each end. Sew to bottom of quilt.

5. Add wide side and bottom borders, mitering lower corners and trimming excess from seams. Add narrow top border.
6. In one half of a folded square of tracing paper, trace the quilting motif given on page 81. Rotate the paper, and trace again on the other half to complete motif. Mark the motif in each A patch.
7. Trace ¾ of the flower from complete quilting motif over miters at lower border corners. Measure and mark a line with tailor's chalk ⁹⁄₁₆" in from outer seam line of side and bottom borders. In the bottom border, mark 17 of the leaf motifs (shown in gray on the half-block quilting pattern) matching dot to dot along the marked line. Similarly mark 22 motifs along each side border. Quilt as marked. Quilt "in the ditch" or outline quilt ¼" from seam lines around colored C's and around the stair-stepped muslin shapes. Bind in red to finish.

Arrows in pattern pieces indicate straight of grain.

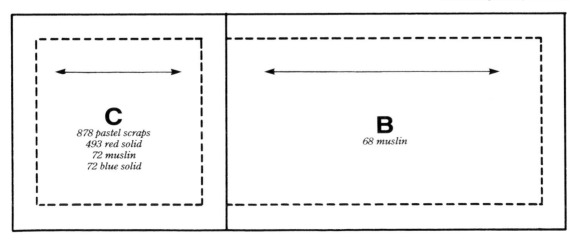

C
878 pastel scraps
493 red solid
72 muslin
72 blue solid

B
68 muslin

BLOCK Z

		Red	Mu	Red		
			Red			
Red			Blue			Red
Mu	Red	Blue		Blue	Red	Mu
Red			Blue			Red
			Red			
		Red	Mu	Red		

BLOCK Z PIECING

C	C	C	C	C	C	C
C	C	C	C	C	C	C
C	C	C	C	C	C	C
C	C	C	C	C	C	C
C	C	C	C	C	C	C
C	C	C	C	C	C	C
C	C	C	C	C	C	C

Red			**UNIT 1**
	Red		**UNIT 2**
			UNIT 3

*Arrows in pattern pieces
indicate straight of grain.*

BLOCK Y

	Red	Muslin	Red	
Red				Red
Muslin		Muslin		Muslin
Red				Red
	Red	Muslin	Red	

BLOCK Y PIECING

C	C	B	C	C
C				C
B		A		B
C				C
C	C	B	C	C

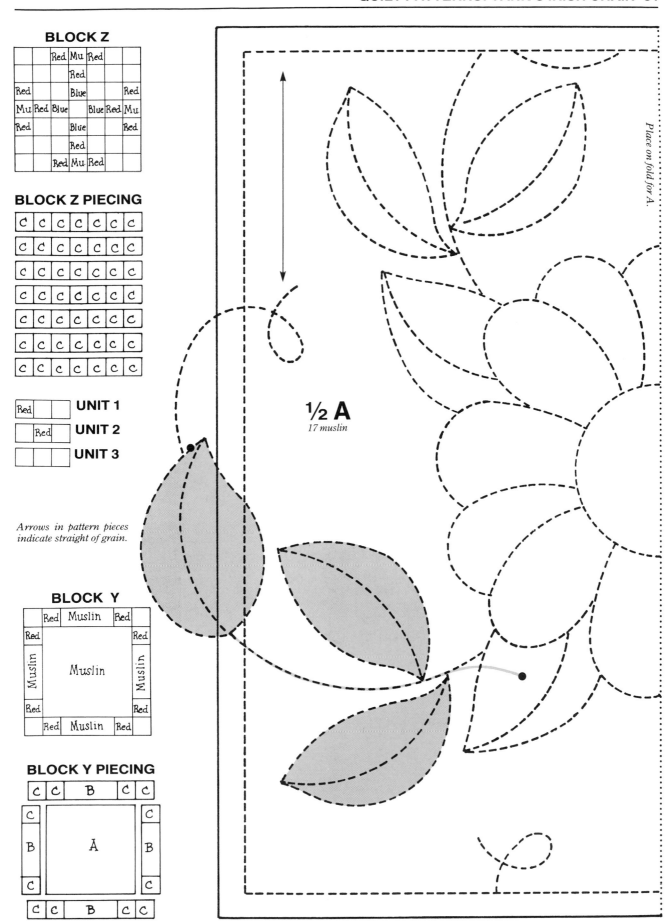

Place on fold for A.

½ **A**
17 muslin

COUNTRY COUSIN

A simple counterchange of red and white, this new pattern evokes the old Robbing Peter to Pay Paul designs. A sawtooth border completes the image. Easy enough for a beginner, this quilt can be pieced by hand or machine and quilted without marking. Country Cousin's color photograph is on page 64.

MATERIALS NEEDED

Block Size: 8". Quilt Size: 78" x 94".

2¾ yds.	**Medium Red Print:** 2 borders 3½" x 96½", 2 borders 3½" x 80½".
¾ yd.	**Dark Red Solid:** binding 1½" x 10¼ yds.
2¼ yds.	**Cream Print:** 2 borders 2½" x 78½", 2 borders 2½" x 62½"
4 yds.	**or Scraps in Various Red Prints:** 198 A, 640 B.
4¼ yds.	**or Scraps in Various Light Prints:** 190 A, 632 B, 4 C, 4 D, 4 E, 4 F.
5⅝ yds.	**Lining. 82" x 98" Batting.**

    1. Referring to block drawing and piecing diagram, make 63 blocks. Be careful to press all seams toward the darker fabric.

    2. Join blocks into 9 rows of 7 blocks each. Join rows.

    3. Add cream borders, mitering corners and trimming excess from seam allowances.

    4. Make inner pieced border as follows: Join a light and a red B to make a square Unit 1. Repeat to make 128 Unit 1's. Sew two red B's to a light D to make a rectangular Unit 2. Repeat to make 4 Unit 2's. Sew 14 Unit 1's to each short side of a Unit 2, being careful to turn Unit 1's at center of border as shown in the quilt photo. Sew to top of quilt. Repeat for bottom of quilt.

Sew 18 of the remaining Unit 1's to each short end of another Unit 2, being careful to turn squares properly. Sew a light E to each end. Sew to side of quilt. Repeat for other side.

    5. Similarly make outer pieced border: Join a red A to a light A to make Unit 3. Make 64 Unit 3's. Join two red A's to a light C to make a rectangular Unit 4. Repeat to make four Unit 4's. Sew 7 Unit 3's to each short side of Unit 4. Sew to top of quilt. Repeat for bottom of quilt. Sew 9 Unit 3's to each short side of another Unit 4. Sew a light F to each end. Sew to side of quilt. Repeat for other side.

    6. Add red borders, mitering corners and trimming excess from seam allowances.

    7. Outline quilt or quilt "in the ditch" along all seam lines. Bind in red solid to finish.

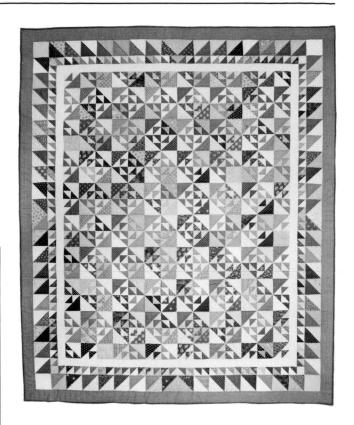

BLOCK
BLOCK PIECING

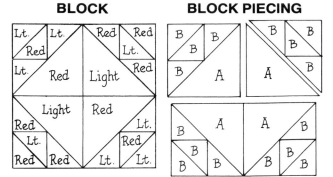

CORNER DIAGRAM

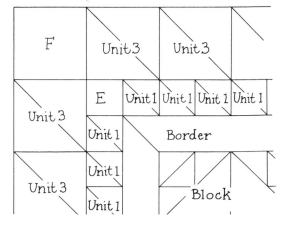

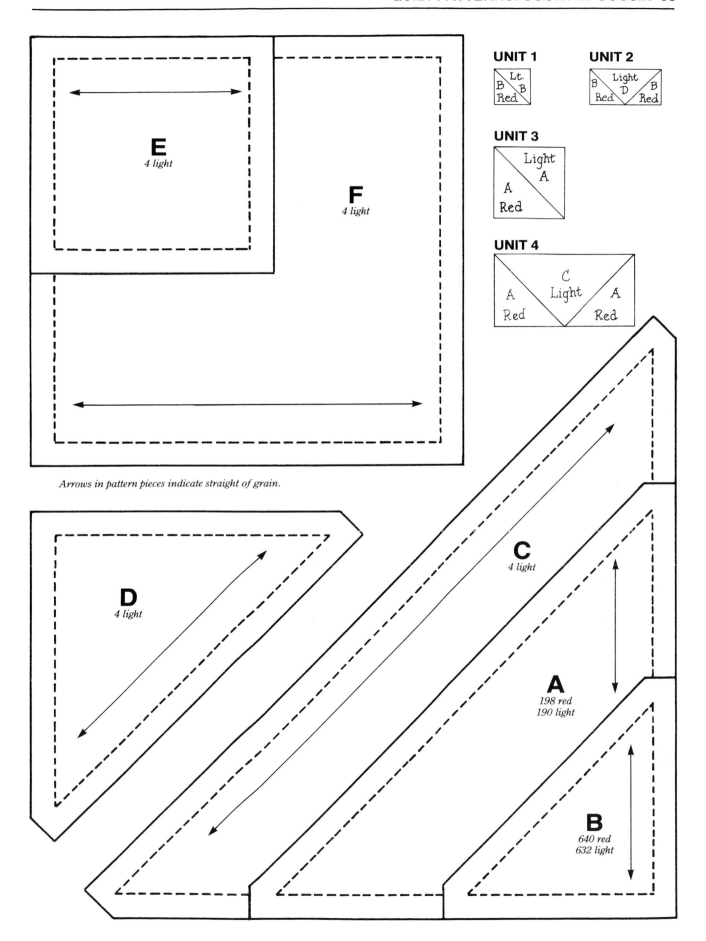

E
4 light

F
4 light

UNIT 1
B | Lt. | B
Red

UNIT 2
B | Light | B
Red | D | Red

UNIT 3
Light
A
A
Red

UNIT 4
C
Light
A | A
Red | Red

Arrows in pattern pieces indicate straight of grain.

D
4 light

C
4 light

A
198 red
190 light

B
640 red
632 light

BLOCK PATTERNS

Many traditional patterns (whether or not they are usually made from scraps) make lovely scrap quilts. In the next nine pages, 72 traditional blocks are presented. For each block, color ideas and a quilt setting arrangement, with dimensions, are suggested. Feel free, of course, to vary these ideas for your quilt. Be sure to add to the quilt dimensions listed any borders you may desire. A lettered piecing diagram is given beside each block. The letters refer to the full-size pattern pieces on pages 94-96, which you can use to make any of the quilts in this section. Refer to the chapter, "How to Make a Quilt," on pages 24-28 for basic quiltmaking techniques.

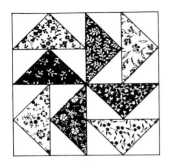 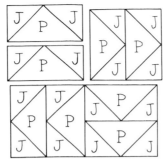

Dutchman's Puzzle, 8″

80 blocks set 8 x 10 with 1½″ sashes make a quilt 77½″ x 96½″. Make each block from an assortment of scraps set off by a plain background for an old-fashioned look.

Puss in the Corner, 8″

Stretch your collection of scraps with plain alternate blocks in this easy quilt. 50 pieced blocks alternated with 49 plain squares form a quilt 72″ x 88″ (set 9 x 11).

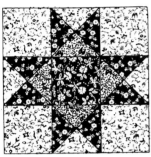 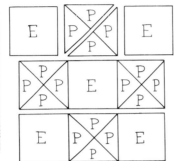

Ohio Star, 12″

42 blocks (each in a different set of coordinated fabrics) set 6 x 7 with 2″ sashes make a quilt 86″ x 100″. Change the light/dark placement from block to block, if desired.

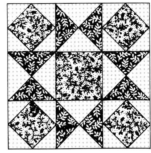 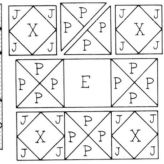

Combination Star, 12″

Try using the same fabric for the star points and sashes throughout the quilt and varying the other patches. 35 blocks set 5 x 7 with 1½″ sashes make a quilt 69″ x 96″.

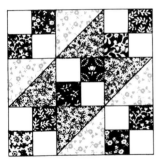 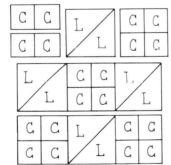

Jacob's Ladder, 12″

48 blocks set side by side in 8 rows of 6 blocks make a quilt 72″ x 96″. Use different dark scraps but use the same medium print in each block to enhance the overall pattern.

 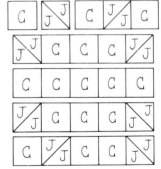

Sister's Choice, 10″

Within a planned color scheme, coordinate different fabrics for each block. 56 blocks set 7 x 8 with 2″ sashes make a quilt 86″ x 98″ before borders.

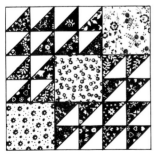 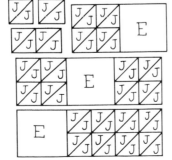

Cut Glass Dish, 12″

Choose medium and dark scraps in your favorite color. 18 pieced blocks alternated with 17 plain quilted squares (set 5 x 7) with 6″ quilted borders make a quilt 72″ x 96″.

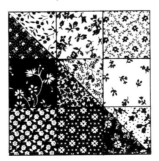 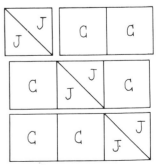

Nine-Patch Variation, 6″

Use a wide variety of small scraps in lights and darks to make this easy Log Cabin-look quilt. 192 blocks set 12 x 16 make a quilt 72″ x 96″.

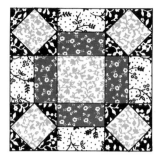 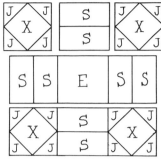

Rolling Stone, 12″

This makes a pretty monochromatic quilt in several shades of your favorite color. 42 blocks set 6 x 7 with 1½″ sashes make a quilt 82½″ x 96″ before borders.

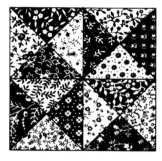 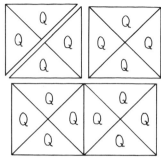

Yankee Puzzle, 12″

Try using all different prints in each block, whether you stick to a color scheme or a multicolored look. 42 blocks set 6 x 7 with 2″ sashes make a quilt 86″ x 100″.

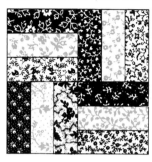 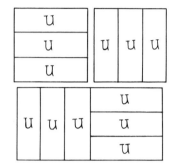

Roman Stripe, 9″

Choose three colors, and keep their placement the same in each block. Use many different prints for each color, though. 80 blocks set 8 x 10 make a quilt 72″ x 90″.

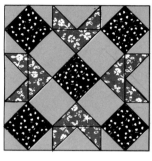 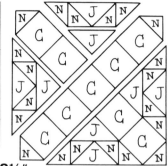

Swing in the Center, 8½″

Try making each block from different prints, but with the solids the same throughout. 63 blocks set 7 x 9 with 2″ sashes make a quilt 75½″ x 96½″.

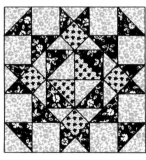 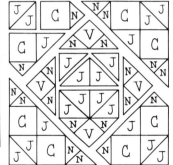

Hill and Crag, 10″

This is pretty in three colors. Use different fabrics for each color in the various blocks. 32 pieced blocks alternated with 31 plain blocks make a quilt 70″ x 90″.

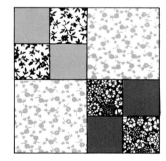 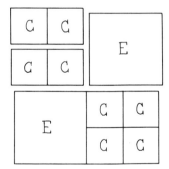

Four Patch, 8″

Make each 4-patch from one print and a matching solid. Use a variety of colors, but use the same print for all the large squares. 88 blocks set 8 x 11 make a quilt 64″ x 88″.

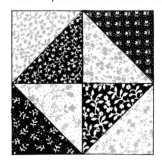 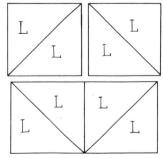

Broken Dishes, 8″

This pattern looks perky in rainbow colors or subdued in a monochromatic color scheme. 99 easy-to-make blocks set 9 x 11 make a quilt 72″ x 88″ before borders.

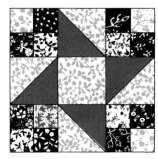 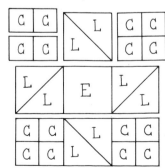

Water Wheel, 12″

Make the dark triangles from a different solid in each block and make the 4-patches from a variety of prints. 56 blocks set 7 x 8 make a quilt 84″ x 96″.

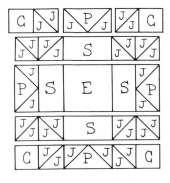

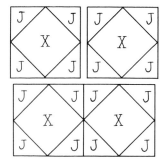

Arizona, 12″

This pattern makes a pretty quilt with each block similar in color, though using different prints. 42 blocks set 6 x 7 with 2″ sashes make a quilt 86″ x 100″.

Broken Sash, 8″

Use a large variety of scrap prints for the triangles. Vary the four solid squares from block to block. 63 blocks set 7 x 9 with 2″ sashes make a quilt 72″ x 92″.

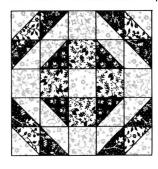
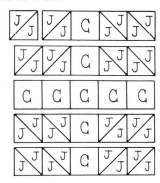

Variable Star, 8″

Choose a color scheme, and within its limitations make each block as different as possible. 50 pieced blocks set alternately with 49 plain blocks make a quilt 72″ x 88″.

Wedding Ring, 10″

Choose a color scheme, such as rust, brown, green, and gold, and vary the combinations for the blocks. 42 blocks set 6 x 7 with 2″ sashes make a quilt 74″ x 86″.

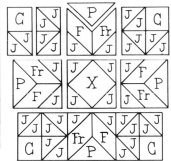
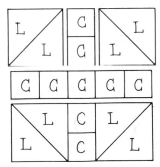
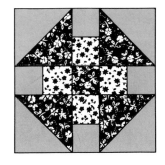

Wyoming Valley Block, 12″

Choose six or eight colors, and combine them differently for each block. 18 pieced blocks alternated with 17 plain squares make a quilt 60″ x 84″ (set 5 x 7).

Churn Dash, 10″

This pattern is pretty with the same solid throughout and different prints in just two colors. 32 pieced blocks set alternately with 31 plain blocks make a quilt 70″ x 90″.

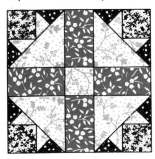
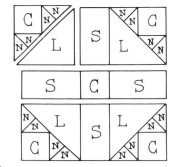
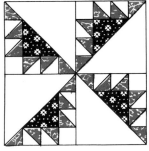
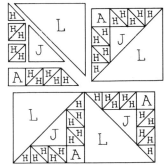

Cross and Crown, 10″

Use light and dark print scraps of a single color, browns ranging into rusts and blacks, perhaps. 41 pieced blocks alternated with 40 plain blocks make a quilt 90″ x 90″.

Kansas Troubles, 8″

An assortment of crisp, dark colors against muslin, with a different dark print in each block, looks handsome in this pattern. 80 blocks set 8 x 10 make a quilt 64″ x 80″.

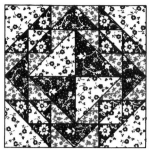 

Corn and Beans, 12"

This quilt is pretty in an assortment of greens, golds, and browns, combined differently for each block. 35 blocks set 5 x 7 with 1½" sashes make a quilt 69" x 96".

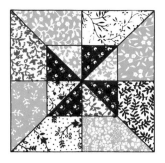 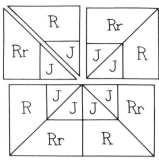

Double Windmill, 8"

This makes a pretty quilt in multicolored pastels. Make the pinwheels brighter for a colorful focal point in each block. 108 blocks set 9 x 12 make a quilt 72" x 96".

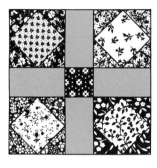 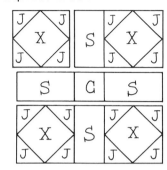

Economy, 10"

A wide variety of prints perks up this simple pattern. Make the solid rectangles the same throughout. 35 blocks set 5 x 7 with 2" sashes make a quilt 62" x 86" before borders.

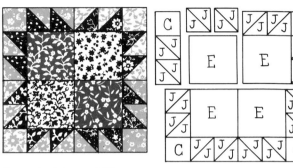

Crow's Foot, 12"

Try making this quilt entirely of scraps in a multitude of clear, bright colors. 42 blocks set 6 x 7 with 2" sashes make a quilt 86" x 100".

 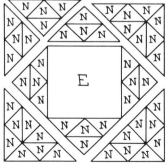

Our Village Green, 8"

Decide on a color scheme, and select a variety of prints for each block, keeping the solids the same. 50 pieced blocks alternated with 49 plain blocks make a quilt 72" x 88".

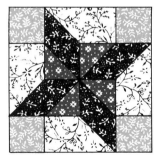 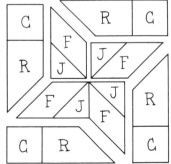

Clay's Choice, 8"

Choose a scheme of four colors, and make each block from different fabrics in the same color placement. 72 blocks set 8 x 9 with 2" sashes make a quilt 82" x 92".

 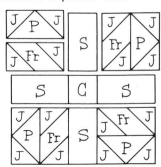

Birds in the Air, 6"

This looks pretty in several shades of one color. Use the same fabric throughout for the large triangles. 192 blocks set 12 x 16 make a quilt 72" x 96".

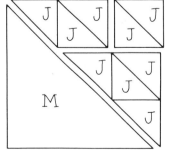 

Jack in the Box, 10"

Choose a different pair of prints in closely related shades for each block. 32 pieced blocks set alternately with 31 plain blocks make a quilt 70" x 90" (set 7 x 9).

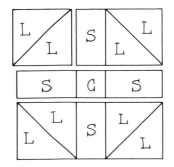 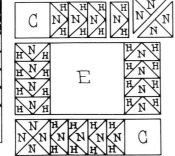

Shoofly, 10″

This pattern is pretty in a rainbow of colors with each block made from a different pair of prints. 48 blocks set 6 x 8 with 2″ sashes make a quilt 74″ x 98″.

Double X, 12″

This is an old-fashioned beauty no matter how you color the scraps. 18 pieced blocks set alternately with 17 plain ones make a quilt 60″ x 84″ (set 5 x 7).

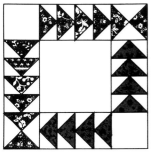 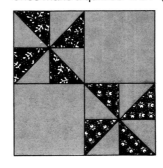

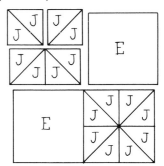

Wild Goose Chase, 8″

This quilt is super in a monochromatic color scheme or in bright multicolors. 50 pieced blocks set alternately with 49 plain squares make a quilt 72″ x 88″ (set 9 x 11).

Pinwheels, 12″

Make each pinwheel using a different dark scrap, but use the same light solid throughout. 88 blocks set side by side 8 x 11 make a quilt 64″ x 88″.

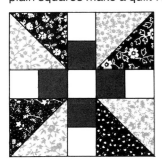 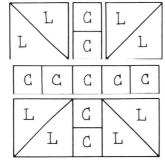

 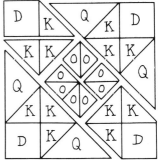

Propeller, 10″

Use scraps for the triangles, but use the same solids for the squares throughout. 63 blocks set 7 x 9 with 1″ sashing make a quilt 78″ x 100″.

Martha Washington Star, 12″

This is a natural for red, white, and blue. Make some blocks with red stars and others with blue stars. 42 blocks set 6 x 7 with 1½″ sashing make a quilt 82½″ x 96″.

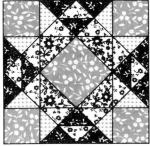 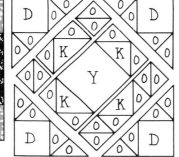

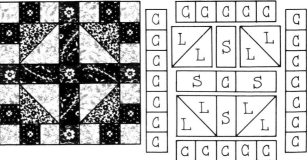

Georgetown Circle, 12″

Choose several colors you like together, and from these choose a few fabrics for each block. 32 pieced blocks alternated with 31 plain ones make a quilt 84″ x 108″.

Lincoln's Platform, 14″

Reverse the placement of light and dark scrap patches around neighboring blocks for a handsome checkerboard effect. 42 blocks set 6 x 7 make a quilt 84″ x 98″.

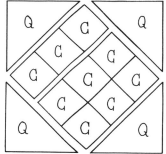

Crossroads to Jericho, 8½″
Make each nine-patch from different prints, with the large triangles the same throughout. 50 pieced blocks set alternately with 49 plain blocks make a quilt 76½″ x 93½″.

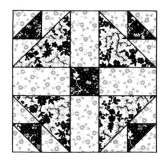
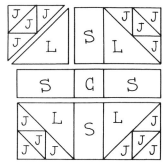

Fox and Geese, 10″
Try choosing a color scheme of up to six colors and making the blocks from various combinations of them. 48 blocks set 6 x 8 with 2″ sashes make a quilt 74″ x 98″.

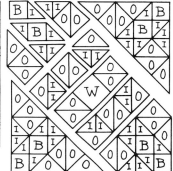

Indian Maze, 12″
Select several shades of one color: blue, red, brown, green, or whatever you like. 18 pieced blocks alternated with 17 plain blocks make a quilt 60″ x 84″ (set 5 x 7).

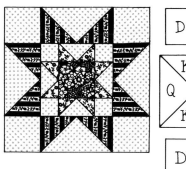

Rising Star, 12″
For a real beauty, choose a color scheme and vary the blocks within that range. 56 blocks set side by side 7 x 8 make a quilt 84″ x 96″.

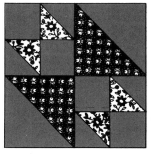
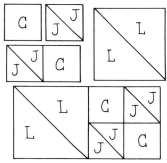

Old Maid's Puzzle, 8″
Choose an old-fashioned color scheme like turkey red, brown, gold, teal blue and black for a stunning traditional quilt. 110 blocks set 10 x 11 make a quilt 80″ x 88″.

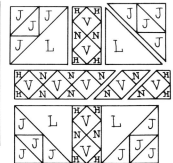

Bird's Nest, 10″
From a scheme of about six colors, combine three or four fabrics for each different block. 48 blocks set 6 x 8 with 2″ sashing make a quilt 74″ x 98″.

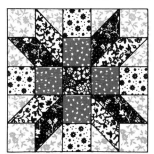
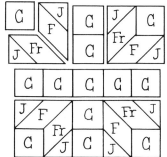

Miller's Daughter, 10″
Use assorted fabrics in a half-dozen colors. Combine prints differently for each block. 32 pieced blocks alternated with 31 plain blocks make a quilt 70″ x 90″.

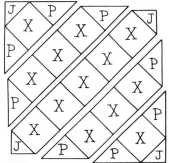

Grandmother's Pride, 12″
Match the four solid squares in the center of each block to the sashing for continuity. 35 blocks set 5 x 7 with 2″ sashing make a quilt 72″ x 100″.

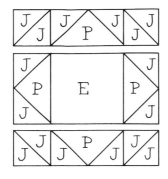 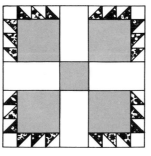

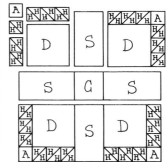

The Cypress, 8″

This looks pretty in a monochromatic scheme or in multicolors. 80 blocks set 8 x 10 make a quilt 64″ x 80″ (77½″ x 96½″ if set with 1½″ sashes).

Premium Star, 10″

Try an assortment of pastels for the large squares and brights for the small triangles on a muslin background. 56 blocks set 7 x 8 with 1″ sashes make a quilt 78″ x 89″.

 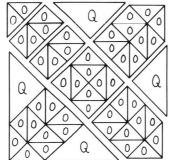

 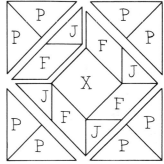

Old Maid's Ramble, 12″

This quilt can be stunning in a monochromatic scheme or in several colors, with color placement different for each block. 48 blocks set 6 x 8 make a quilt 72″ x 96″.

Windblown Star, 8″

Use an assortment of scraps for the triangles in the block corners; these make pinwheels where neighboring blocks meet. 88 blocks set 8 x 11 make a quilt 64″ x 88″.

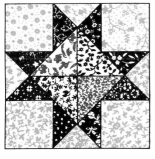 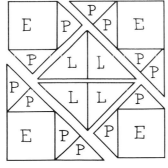

 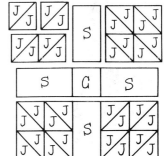

Country Farm, 12″

Make each block a potpourri of scraps for an old-fashioned effect. 35 blocks set 5 x 7 with 2″ sashes make a quilt 72″ x 100″ before borders.

Handy Andy, 10″

This is especially lovely in blue or turkey red and muslin. 32 pieced blocks alternated with 31 plain blocks make a quilt 70″ x 90″ (set 7 x 9).

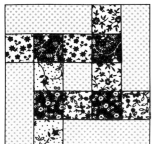 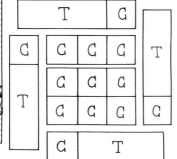

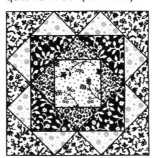 

Flying Squares, 7½″

This makes a pretty multicolored quilt with a variety of prints in each block. 48 blocks set 6 x 8 with 2″ sashes make a quilt 74″ x 98″.

Gentleman's Fancy, 12″

This pattern is perfect for multicolored scraps. 18 pieced blocks alternated with 17 plain blocks make a quilt 60″ x 84″ (set 5 x 7).

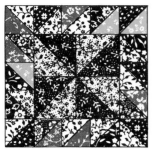
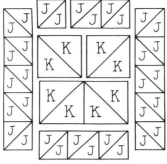

Unnamed, 10″

This pattern makes a handsome quilt in dark, warm shades accented with red. 56 blocks set 7 x 8 with 1″ sashing make a quilt 78″ x 89″.

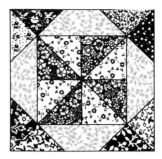
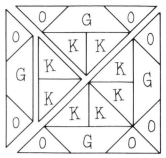

The Range's Pride, 8″

Make the center pinwheel of a block from just two fabrics, but use all different fabrics for the block's corners. 80 blocks set 8 x 10 make a quilt 72″ x 90″.

Duck and Ducklings Variation, 12″

Try using a variety of prints in each block, whether you stick to a color scheme or make the quilt multicolored. 42 blocks set 6 x 7 with 1½″ sashes make a quilt 82½″ x 96″.

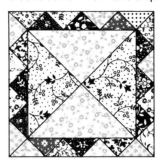
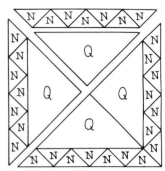

Aunt Mary's Double Irish Chain, 8″

Use the same two fabrics for the large triangles throughout the quilt, but select a wide variety of scraps for the small triangles. 99 blocks set 9 x 11 make a quilt 72″ x 88″.

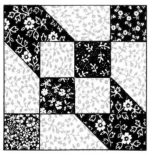
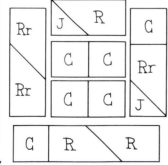

Road to Oklahoma, 8″

Try a three-color scheme with each block utilizing a number of prints for a handsome effect. 99 blocks set 9 x 11 make a quilt 72″ x 88″.

Union, 12″

This pattern is particularly striking in an old-fashioned color scheme of red, white, and blue or red and green. 42 blocks set 6 x 7 with 2″ sashing make a quilt 86″ x 100″.

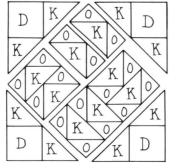

Crazy Ann, 12″

This is a great quilt for scraps in two or three colors. 42 blocks set 6 x 7 with 1″ sashes make a quilt 79″ x 92″ before borders.

Star and Pinwheels, 12″

Within your color scheme, choose three or four fabrics for each different block. 32 pieced blocks set alternately with 31 plain blocks make a quilt 84″ x 108″ (set 7 x 9).

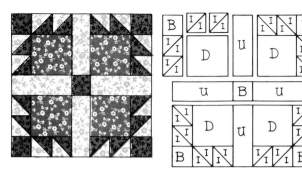

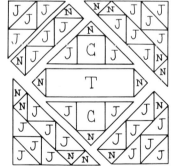

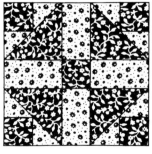

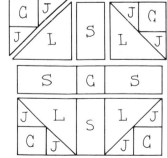

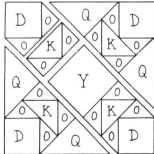

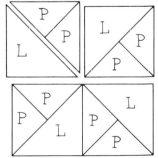

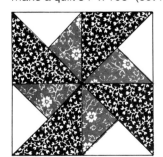

Around the Corner, 12″

Choose a rainbow of bright colors, and make each block different for a lively quilt. 56 blocks set 7 x 8 make a quilt 84″ x 96″ before borders.

Starry Paths, 8″

This quilt looks good in multicolored scraps or in just two colors. Use the same two fabrics for the large triangles throughout. 88 blocks set 8 x 11 make a quilt 64″ x 88″.

Memory Block, 10″

A friendship quilt of blocks, each embroidered with the maker's name, is perfect for scraps. 48 blocks set 6 x 8 with 2″ sashes make a quilt 74″ x 98″.

Grandmother's Choice, 10″

Make each block from a different pair of prints in either a monochromatic or multicolored scheme. 32 pieced blocks alternated with 31 plain blocks make a quilt 70″ x 90″.

Dove in the Window, 10½″

Make each block from a different set of fabrics in basically the same colors. 72 blocks set 8 x 9 make a quilt 84″ x 94½″ before borders.

Spinning Stars, 8″

This is a spectacular monochromatic quilt. Choose an assortment of prints or just one fabric and muslin for each block. 108 blocks set 9 x 12 make a quilt 72″ x 96″.

Northumberland Star, 12″

Try using a different set of coordinating fabrics for each block. 32 pieced blocks alternated with 31 plain blocks make a quilt 84″ x 108″ (set 7 x 9).

Windmill, 8″

Two shades of the same color give this block a 3-D look. Use different pairs of fabrics for each block. 80 blocks set 8 x 10 with 1½″ sashing make a quilt 77½″ x 96½″.

FULL-SIZE BLOCK PATTERNS. The patterns here and on the next two pages can be used to make quilts from the 72 blocks shown on pages 85-93. Dashed lines indicate seam lines. Solid lines indicate cutting lines. Where a larger pattern piece is overlapped by a smaller one, be sure to include the extension plus the entire portion covered by the smaller patch when you make the template for the larger pattern piece. Grain lines are not shown here because they may vary, depending on which block you are making. See "How to Make a Quilt," pages 24-28 for information about grain lines, making templates, and other helpful subjects.

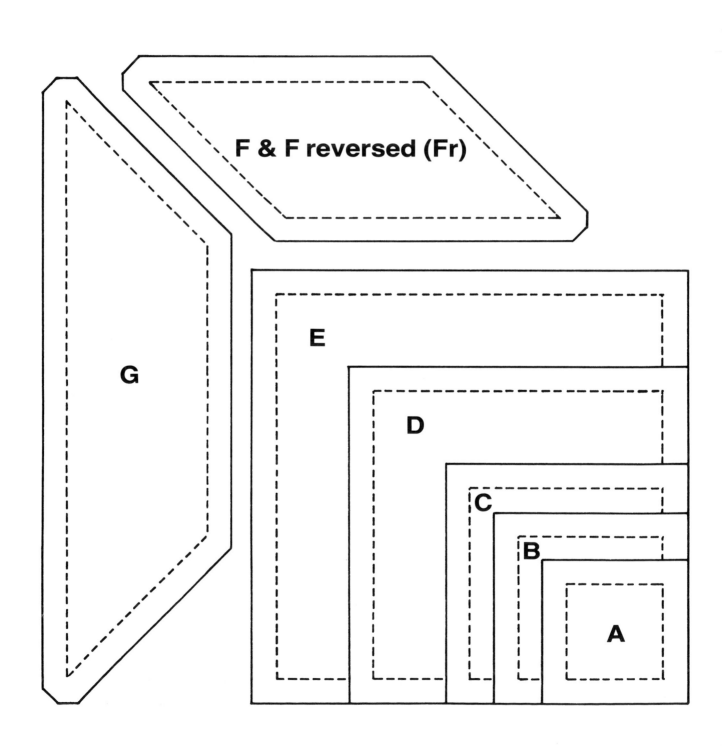

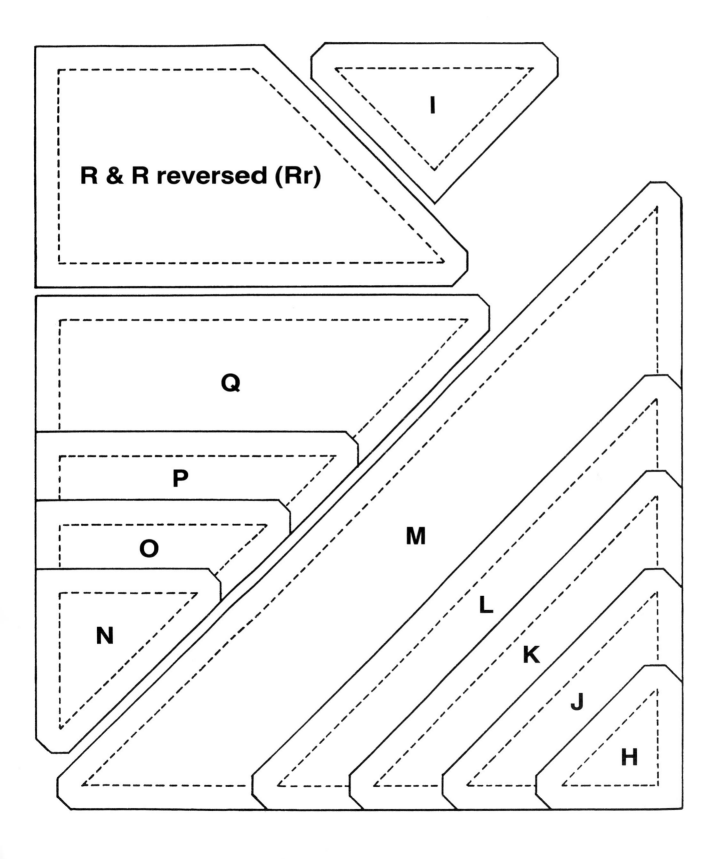

R & R reversed (Rr)

I

Q

P

O

N

M

L

K

J

H

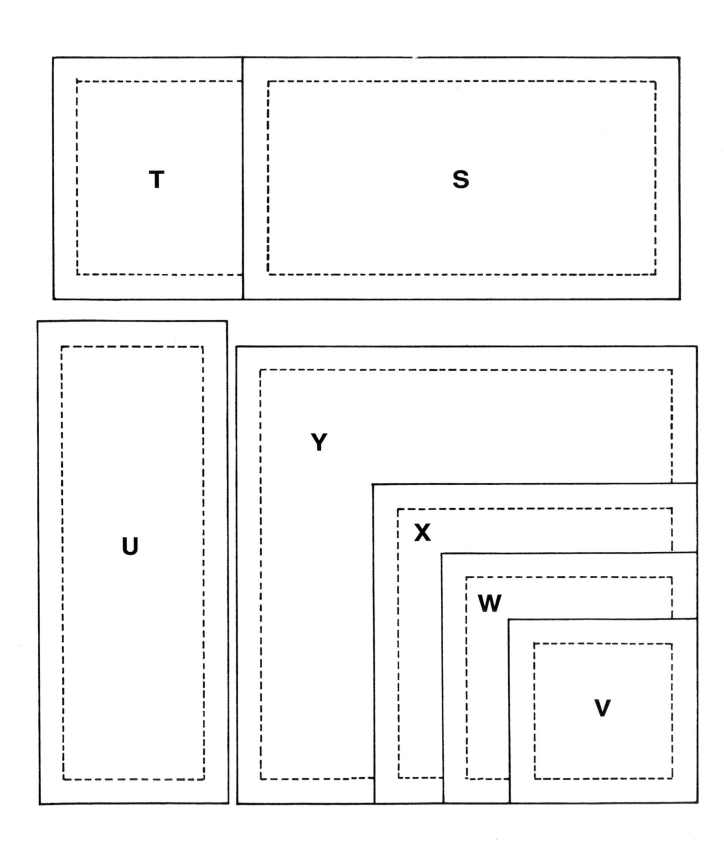